Discover Beading

Compiled by Lesley Weiss

Printed in the United States of America

10 09 08 07 06   1 2 3 4 5

Publisher's Cataloging-In-Publication Data
(Prepared by The Donohue Group, Inc.)

Discover beading / compiled by Lesley Weiss.

    p., : col. ill. ; cm.

    Includes index.
    All projects have appeared previously in BeadStyle magazine, except for Classic knotted pearls and Easy macramé choker.

    ISBN-13: 978-0-87116-239-7
    ISBN-10: 0-87116-239-3

1. Beadwork--Handbooks, manuals, etc. 2. Beadwork--Patterns. 3. Jewelry making--Handbooks, manuals, etc. I. Weiss, Lesley. II. Title: BeadStyle Magazine.

TT860 .D57 2006
745.594/2

Acknowledgments: Linda Augsburg, Beth Bakkum, Lisa Bergman, Paulette Biedenbender, Mindy Brooks, Karin Buckingham, Melanie Buellesbach, Jim Forbes, Naomi Fujimoto, Lindsay Haedt, Judith Hill, Cathy Jakicic, Kelly Katlaps, Jane Konkel, Pat Lantier, Lisa Mooney, Salena Safranski, Kristin Schneidler, Kristin Sutter, Mark Thompson, Helene Tsigistras, Annette Wall, Lesley Weiss, Bill Zuback

These designs are for your personal use. They are not intended for resale.
All projects have appeared previously in *BeadStyle* magazine, except "Classic knotted pearls" and "Easy macramé choker."

ꓛONTENTS

PLIERS AND CUTTERS

bentnose pliers

chainnose pliers

roundnose pliers

crimping pliers

split ring pliers

diagonal wire cutters

STRINGING MATERIALS

twisted wire

flexible beading wire

beading thread/cord

memory wire

sterling silver wire

leather beading cord

How to choose flexible beading wire for a project

The .012, .014, and .015 wire descriptions refer to the different diameters of beading wire. For example, .012 wire measures .012 inches in diameter. The weight and design of your project will determine the choice of wire. Generally, use .010 or .012 to string lightweight or small-holed beads; .014 or .015 for most gemstones, crystals, and glass beads; and .018, .019, or .024 to string heavy beads or nuggets. Additionally, wire comes in different strand quantities: 7, 19, 21, and 49. This refers to the number of wires entwined to comprise the diameter. The more strands, the more pliable the wire and the less likely it is that the wire will kink.

FINDINGS

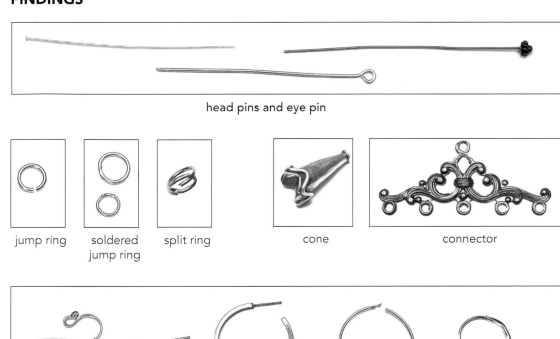

head pins and eye pin

jump ring

soldered
jump ring

split ring

cone

connector

earring findings

clasps

bead tips

crimp beads
and crimp covers

crimp ends

spacers

CRIMPING

Flat crimp

1 Hold the crimp using the tip of your chainnose pliers. Squeeze the pliers firmly to flatten the crimp.

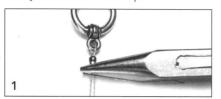

2 Tug the wire to make sure the crimp has a solid grip. If the wire slides, repeat the steps with a new crimp.

How to choose crimp sizes and crimping methods

Both flat and folded crimps provide a strong hold. Folded crimps are preferred when the crimp is noticeable. Also, a folded crimp can slide easily into a large-holed bead for a polished finish. When you make a folded crimp, make sure the wires are separated within the crimp as you make the first fold. Most jewelry can be finished with 1 x 2mm tube crimps. Micro crimps are designed for finer wire or to keep beads stable on illusion necklaces. Flatten a micro crimp with chainnose pliers or use a special tool made for micro crimping.

Folded crimp

1 Position the crimp bead in the notch closest to the crimping pliers' handle.

2 Separate the wires and firmly squeeze the crimp.

3 Move the crimp into the notch at the pliers' tip and hold the crimp as shown. Squeeze the crimp bead, folding it in half at the indentation.

4 Test that the folded crimp is secure.

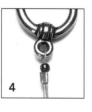

End crimp

Folded crimp ends, sometimes called bookend crimps, are used to connect leather or satin cord to a clasp.
1 Glue one end of the cord and place it in a crimp end. Use chainnose pliers to fold one side of the crimp end over the cord.

2 Repeat on the second side and squeeze gently. Test to be sure the crimp end is secure.

Crimp covers

Crimp covers can add a professional look to your jewelry. Cup the crimp cover around the crimped crimp bead and gently close with chainnose pliers or the notch near the tip of your crimping pliers.

LOOPS AND JUMP RINGS

Opening and closing loops and jump rings

1 Hold the loop or jump ring with two pairs of chainnose pliers or chainnose and roundnose pliers, as shown.
2 To open the loop or jump ring, bring one pair of pliers toward you and push the other pair away.

3 String materials on the open loop or jump ring. Reverse the steps to close the open loop or jump ring.

Plain loops

1 Trim the wire or head pin ⅜ in. (1cm) above the top bead. Make a right angle bend close to the bead.
2 Grab the wire's tip with roundnose pliers. The tip of the wire should be flush with the pliers. Roll the wire to form a half circle. Release the wire.

3 Reposition the pliers in the loop and continue rolling.
4 The finished loop should form a centered circle above the bead.

Wrapped loops

1 Make sure you have at least 1¼ in. (3.2cm) of wire above the bead. With the tip of your chainnose pliers, grasp the wire directly above the bead. Bend the wire (above the pliers) into a right angle.
2 Using roundnose pliers, position the jaws in the bend as shown.

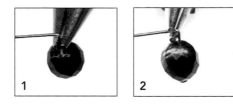

3 Bring the wire over the top jaw of the roundnose pliers.
4 Reposition the pliers' lower jaw snugly in the loop. Curve the wire downward around the bottom of the roundnose pliers. This is the first half of a wrapped loop.

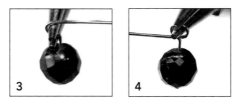

5 Position the chainnose pliers' jaws across the loop.
6 Wrap the wire around the wire stem, covering the stem between the loop and the top bead. Trim the excess wire and press the cut end close to the wraps.

BASIC TECHNIQUES

DISCOVER BEADING **7**

KNOTS

Overhand knot
Make a loop and pass the working end through it. Pull the ends to tighten the knot.

Square knot
1 Cross the right-hand cord over the left-hand cord, and then bring it under the left-hand cord from back to front. Pull it up in front so both ends are pointing upward.

2 Cross right over left, forming a loop, and go through the loop, again from back to front. Pull the ends to tighten the knot.

Surgeon's knot
Cross the right end over the left end and go through the loop. Go through again. Pull the ends to tighten. Cross the left end over the right end and go through once. Pull the ends to tighten.

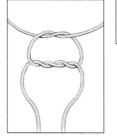

Lark's head knot
Fold a cord in half and lay it behind a ring, loop, bar, etc. with the fold pointing down. Bring the ends through the ring from back to front then through the fold and tighten.

Macramé square knot
1 Cross the right-hand cord over the center cords and under the left-hand cord. Bring the left-hand cord under the center cords and through the loop formed by the right-hand cord from back to front. Keeping the center cords flat, tighten the outer cords.
2 Cross the left-hand cord over the center cords and under the right-hand cord. Bring the right-hand cord under the center cords and through the loop of the left-hand cord from back to front. Tighten.

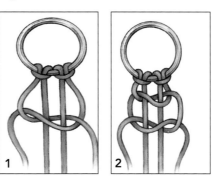

How many beads per inch?

Bead size	3mm	4mm	5mm	6mm	8mm	10mm	12mm
# beads/in.	8.25	6.25	5.0	4.25	3.25	2.5	2.0

BASIC TECHNIQUES

STRINGING

Stringing may be the easiest beading technique, but that doesn't mean the results are plain or simple. From a single strand of graduated rondelles to a multistrand cuff with shimmering drops, you can create a beautiful array of necklaces, bracelets, and earrings by simply stringing.

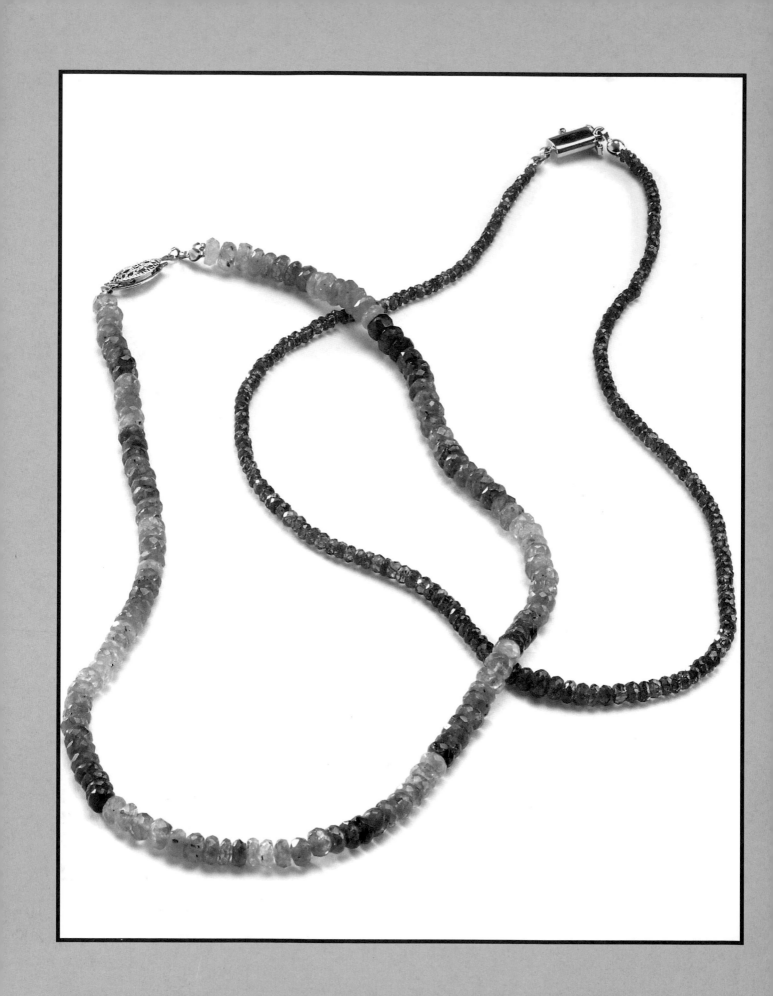

Graduated gemstones

Graduated gemstones create a simple, elegant strand

by Sylvia Sur

When you start with a strand of fine, semi-precious gemstones, such as the faceted spinel shown here, you don't need to add any embellishment to create a beautiful piece of jewelry. Simply string the beads and wear them.

SupplyList

- 14-in. (36-41cm) or longer strand faceted spinel or other fine gemstone
- **2** seed beads, size 11º
- Fireline fishing line, 8-lb. test
- **2** bead tips
- clasp
- chainnose pliers
- diagonal wire cutters
- G-S Hypo Cement

1a Determine the finished length of your necklace (this one is 15¾ in./40cm), add 6 in. (15cm), and cut a piece of Fireline to that length.

1b Transfer the beads from their temporary stringing material (pink thread, lower right) to Fireline (gray strand, upper left).

2 String a bead tip and a seed bead on one end of the Fireline.

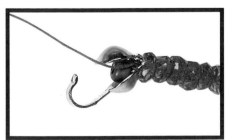

3 Slide the seed bead into the bead tip. Knot the Fireline around the seed bead using several overhand knots (see Basic Techniques, p. 6). Glue the knots.

4 Use chainnose pliers to squeeze the bead tip closed over the seed bead.

5a Attach the bead tip's hook to the loop on one clasp half. Close the hook gently with chainnose pliers.

5b Repeat steps 3 through 5a to finish the other end of the necklace.

Jewel tone bracelets

Dichroic beads glow in an iridescent bracelet

by Eva Kapitany

Take advantage of the many beautiful dichroic beads available to make an easy-to-string bracelet. Vibrant crystals, spaced evenly throughout the piece, boost the beads' brilliance and add a touch of elegance. The bracelet's simple and versatile design makes it a welcome addition to a casual wardrobe or a radiant accessory for evening wear.

SupplyList

both projects
- flexible beading wire, .014 or .015
- chainnose or crimping pliers
- diagonal wire cutters

dichroic and bicone crystal bracelet
- **6** 11 x 12mm dichroic beads (Paula Radke, 800-341-4945, beaduse.com)
- **5** 12mm bicone crystals
- **10** 5 x 6mm silver beads
- **2** 3 x 5mm cone-shaped silver beads
- **2** 3mm round spacer beads
- **2** crimp beads
- toggle clasp

dichroic and crystal cube bracelet
- **6** 9 x 15mm dichroic beads (Dee Howl Beads, 505-772-2634, deehowlbeads@gilanet.com)
- **6** 12mm cube-shaped crystals
- **13** 4 x 5mm silver beads
- **2** 3mm round spacer beads
- **2** crimp beads
- toggle clasp

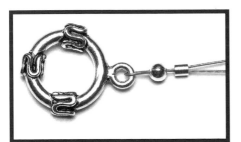

1a Determine the finished length of your bracelet. Add 5 in. (13cm) and cut a piece of beading wire to that length.

1b String a crimp bead, a 3mm round spacer, and half the clasp. Go back through the beads.

EDITOR'S TIP
The use of Aurora Borealis (AB) finish crystals enhances the dichroic beads' iridescent features.

2 String a 5mm cone-shaped bead (if using bicones) or a 4 x 5mm silver bead (if using cubes) to cover the wire's tail.

3 String a dichroic bead, a 5 x 6mm or 4 x 5mm silver bead, a crystal, and a silver bead. Repeat this pattern until the bracelet is within ½ in. (1.3cm) of the desired length. End with a silver bead (cone-shaped bead if stringing bicones). Repeat step 1b with the remaining clasp half. Tighten the wire, check the fit, and add or remove beads from each end if necessary. Crimp the crimp beads (see Basic Techniques, p. 6) and trim the excess wire.

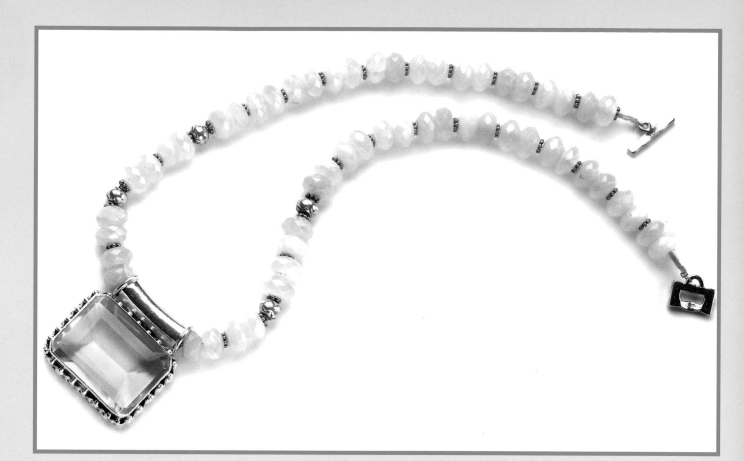

Pendant necklace

Showcase a gorgeous glass pendant with simple faceted rondelles

by Rupa Balachandar

This simple glass pendant shows how gorgeous glass can be. The pendant simulates aquamarine, but at a fraction of the cost. A pendant such as this stands on its own, requiring only complementary beads and a simple pattern to frame it. You'll have a gorgeous necklace and earrings in no time.

1 necklace • Determine the finished length of your necklace (this one is 16 in./41cm), add 6 in. (15cm), and cut a piece of beading wire to that length. String enough seed beads to fill the pendant's bail (hanging loop). Slide the pendant over the beads (this will protect the wire from the bail) and center it on the wire.

2 On each side of the pendant, string two rondelles, a flat spacer, two rondelles, a spacer, a 5mm round bead, and a spacer. Repeat.

3 On each end, string two rondelles interspersed with a flat spacer. Repeat the pattern until you have strung about 7 in. (18cm) of beads on each side.

4 String a flat spacer, a rondelle, a flat spacer, a 3mm round spacer, a crimp bead, a round spacer, and half the clasp on each end. Go back through the last beads strung. Check the fit and add or remove an equal number of beads as necessary. Tighten the wire, crimp the crimp beads (see Basic Techniques, p. 6), and trim the excess wire.

1 earrings • String a flat spacer, a round bead, a spacer, and a rondelle on a head pin.

2 Make a wrapped loop (Basic Techniques) above the top bead. Open the loop on an earring wire and attach the dangle. Close the loop. Make a second earring to match the first.

Supply List

necklace
• glass pendant, approx. 40 x 40mm
• 16-in. (41cm) strand 10 x 5mm faceted rondelles
• **4** 5mm round silver beads
• 1g seed beads, size 11º
• **30** 4mm flat spacers
• **4** 3mm round spacer beads
• flexible beading wire, .014 or .015
• **2** crimp beads
• clasp
• chainnose or crimping pliers
• diagonal wire cutters

earrings
• **2** faceted rondelles left over from necklace
• **4** 4mm flat spacers
• **2** 5mm round silver beads
• **2** 1½-in. (3.8cm) head pins
• pair of earring wires
• chainnose pliers
• roundnose pliers
• diagonal wire cutters

Delicate autumn set

Blend crystal, tourmaline, and topaz for golden warmth

by Naomi Fujimoto

For a touch of shimmer in fall tones, try round dangles mixed with topaz crystal; the warm colors meld beautifully with the yellow-greens and browns of golden tourmaline. Opt for clean lines in the earrings for a set that's complementary but not perfectly matched.

1 **necklace** • String a 6mm round crystal on a head pin. Make a wrapped loop (see Basic Techniques, p. 6) above the bead. Make a total of nine dangles.

2 Determine the finished length of your necklace. (This one is 14½ in./37cm.) Add 6 in. (15cm) and cut a piece of beading wire to that length. Center a dangle on the wire. On each side of the center dangle, string a bicone, a rondelle, a bicone, a rondelle, a bicone, and a dangle. Repeat three more times, then string a bicone. (Alternate groupings of bicone colors, as shown above.)

3 String rondelles on each end until the necklace is within 1 in. (2.5cm) of the desired length.

4 On one end, string a seed bead, a crimp bead, a seed bead, and the clasp. Go back through the last beads strung and tighten the wire. Repeat on the other end, substituting a jump ring for the clasp. Check the fit and add or remove an equal number of beads from each end, if necessary. Crimp the crimp beads (Basic Techniques) and trim the excess wire.

1 **bracelet** • String a round crystal on a head pin and make a plain loop (Basic Techniques) above the bead. Make a total of three dangles and set aside.

2 Determine the finished length of your bracelet, add 5 in. (13cm), and cut two pieces of beading wire to that length. On each strand, string rondelles interspersed with crystals until the bracelet is within 1 in. of the desired length.

3a On one end, string a 3mm round spacer, a crimp bead, a spacer, and the clasp over both strands. Go back through the beads just strung and tighten the wires. Repeat on the other end, substituting a jump ring for the clasp. Check the fit and add or remove beads, if necessary. Crimp the crimp beads and trim the excess wire.

3b Open a dangle's loop and attach it to the jump ring. Close the loop. Repeat with the remaining dangles.

SupplyList

all projects
- chainnose pliers
- roundnose pliers
- diagonal wire cutters

necklace
- 15-in. (38cm) strand 3mm faceted rondelles, golden tourmaline (Dallas Beads and More, 214-761-9596)
- **9** 6mm round crystals, assorted colors to complement the rondelles
- **26** 3mm bicone crystals, **13** each in two colors
- **4** size 11º seed beads
- **9** 1½-in. (3.8cm) head pins
- flexible beading wire, .013 or .014
- **2** crimp beads
- lobster claw clasp and soldered jump ring
- crimping pliers (optional)

bracelet
- 15-in. strand 3mm faceted rondelles, golden tourmaline
- **3** 6mm round crystals
- **10–15** 3mm bicone crystals, two colors
- **4** 3mm round spacer beads
- flexible beading wire, .013 or .014
- **3** 1-in. (2.5cm) or longer head pins
- **2** crimp beads
- lobster claw clasp and soldered jump ring
- crimping pliers (optional)

earrings
- leftover golden tourmaline rondelles
- **2** 3mm bicone crystals
- **2** 1½-in. head pins
- pair of earring wires

1 **earrings** • String rondelles and crystals on a head pin. Leaving space above the top bead, make a wrapped loop.

2 Open the loop on an earring wire and attach the dangle. Close the loop. Make a second earring to match the first.

Pearly summer set

String a summery necklace of free-form mother-of-pearl beads

by Rupa Balachandar

Summer is all about casual confidence and showing some skin. Perfect against a summer tan, these organic mother-of-pearl shards need only a few accent beads to form a captivating collar. Earrings in an earthy hue are equally uncomplicated. Possessing both style and substance, these pieces will take you from the beach to the bistro – effortlessly.

1 **necklace** • Determine the finished length of your necklace (this one is 19 in./48cm), add 6 in. (15cm), and cut a piece of beading wire to that length. Center a spacer, round bead, bead cap, focal bead, bead cap, round bead, and spacer on the wire.

2 On each end, string 2¼ in. (57mm) of mother-of-pearl shards, a spacer, round, and spacer. Repeat the pattern two more times on each end.

3 On one end, string a crimp bead, a seed bead, and half the clasp. Go back through the beads just strung and tighten the wire. Repeat on the other end with the remaining clasp half. Check the fit and add or remove beads, if necessary. Crimp the crimp beads (see Basic Techniques, p. 6) and trim the excess wire.

SupplyList

necklace
- 10 x 12mm focal bead
- 16-in. (41cm) strand mother-of-pearl shards
- **8** 8mm round gemstones, picture jasper
- **14** 5mm daisy spacers
- **2** seed beads, size 11º
- **2** bead caps
- flexible beading wire, .014 or .015
- **2** crimp beads
- clasp
- chainnose or crimping pliers
- diagonal wire cutters

earrings
- **2** 8mm round gemstones, picture jasper
- **2** 3mm Czech fire-polished beads
- **2** 5mm daisy spacers
- **2** 1½-in. (3.8cm) head pins
- pair of earring wires
- chainnose pliers
- roundnose pliers
- diagonal wire cutters

1 **earrings** • String a fire-polished bead, a spacer, and a round bead on a head pin. Make a wrapped loop (Basic Techniques) above the bead.

2 Open the loop on an earring wire and attach the dangle. Close the loop. Make a second earring to match the first.

Opal chip accessories

Capture the iridescent nature of opals in this natural-looking jewelry set

by Naomi Fujimoto

The fresh, organic combination of colors in this set – sky blue opals and earthy brown seed beads – team up in a casual necklace, bracelet, and earrings set.

1a necklace • With roundnose pliers, turn a spiral at one end of a 4-in. (10cm) piece of 20-gauge wire.

1b String an opal pendant on the wire. Make a wrapped loop (see Basic Techniques, p. 6) above the bead.

2a Determine the finished length of your necklace. (The shortest strand of this necklace is 16½ in./42cm; the longest, 17½ in./44cm.) Add 6 in. (15cm) and cut three pieces of beading wire to that length. Center the pendant on one wire.

2b On each side, string approximately 1 in. (2.5cm) of seed beads and a chip. Repeat until the strand is within 1 in. of the desired length, ending with seed beads. This will be the longest strand.

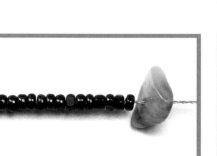

3a On another wire, string 1 in. of seed beads and a chip. Repeat until the strand is ½ in. (1.3cm) shorter than the longest strand. End with seed beads.

3b String the same pattern on the remaining wire, until it is 1 in. shorter than the longest strand.

4 On each end, string a crimp bead, a seed bead, and half the clasp, making sure each strand is positioned correctly. Go back through the last beads strung and tighten the wires. Check the fit and add or remove an equal number of beads from each end, if necessary. Crimp the crimp beads (Basic Techniques) and trim the excess wire.

SupplyList

necklace
- blue opal pendant, approx. 19 x 32mm, vertically drilled
- 16-in. (41cm) strand blue opal chips
- hank of seed beads, size 11º, brown
- 4 in. (10cm) 20-gauge wire
- flexible beading wire, .014 or .015
- **6** crimp beads
- toggle clasp
- chainnose pliers
- roundnose pliers
- diagonal wire cutters
- crimping pliers (optional)

bracelet
- leftover blue opal chips
- leftover seed beads
- flexible beading wire, .014 or .015
- **2** crimp beads
- toggle clasp
- chainnose or crimping pliers
- diagonal wire cutters

earrings
- leftover blue opal chips
- leftover seed beads
- pair of 1-in. (2.5cm) round beading hoops (Fire Mountain Gems, 800-355-2137, firemountaingems.com)
- chainnose pliers

earrings • Intersperse chips with seed beads on a beading hoop. With chainnose pliers, bend the end of the wire hoop up approximately ⅛ in. (3mm) from the end. Make a second earring to match the first.

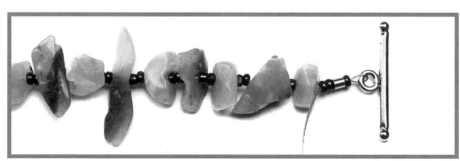

bracelet • Determine the finished length of your bracelet, add 5 in. (13cm), and cut a piece of beading wire to that length. String two seed beads and a chip. Repeat until the strand is within 1 in. of the desired length, ending with two seed beads. On each end, string a crimp bead, a seed bead, and half the clasp. Go back through the last beads strung and tighten the wire. Check the fit and add or remove beads, if necessary. Crimp the crimp beads and trim the excess wire.

Art bead exhibition

Memory wire and rubber tubing provide a great canvas for art beads

by Jean Yates

Using memory wire is so effortless, it's amazing how beautiful the final result can be. When you use art beads with memory wire, that handful of beads you just had to have – but haven't figured out how to showcase – can finally find a worthy backdrop.

Supply List

- **5** 10–20mm art beads
- **7** 8mm beads
- **7** 4mm round crystals
- **7** 4mm bicone crystals
- **4** charms
- **2** size 6º metallic bronze seed beads
- memory wire, bracelet diameter
- **2** 5mm jump rings
- **9.5 in.** (24.1cm) 2.5mm diameter rubber tubing (Rio Grande, 800-545-6566)
- chainnose pliers or heavy-duty wire cutters
- roundnose pliers

1 Separate four coils of memory wire from the stack of coils. Hold the wire with chainnose pliers and bend it back and forth at one place until the wire breaks. You also can use heavy-duty wire cutters. Do not use jewelry-weight wire cutters.

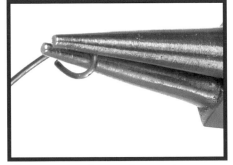

2 Using roundnose pliers, make a small loop on one end of the memory wire.

3 String a round crystal, 8mm bead, bicone crystal, and 2 in. (5cm) of rubber tubing.

4 String an art bead, round, 8mm, bicone, and 1½ in. (3.8cm) of tubing. Repeat this pattern four more times.

5 String a bicone, an 8mm, and a round. Cut the memory wire ¼ in. (6mm) from the last bead. Make a small loop on the end of the wire.

6 Open a jump ring (see Basic Techniques, p. 6) and string a charm, a 6º seed bead, and another charm. Attach the jump ring to a loop at one end of the memory wire and close the jump ring. Make another charm unit and attach it to the loop at the other end of the memory wire.

SUPPLY NOTES
The polymer clay beads used in two of these bracelets are made by Emma Ralph, ejrbeads.co.uk. The pewter charms on those bracelets are from Green Girl Studios, greengirlstudios.com. Leaf charms are available from Fire Mountain Gems, (800) 355-2137, or firemountaingems.com.

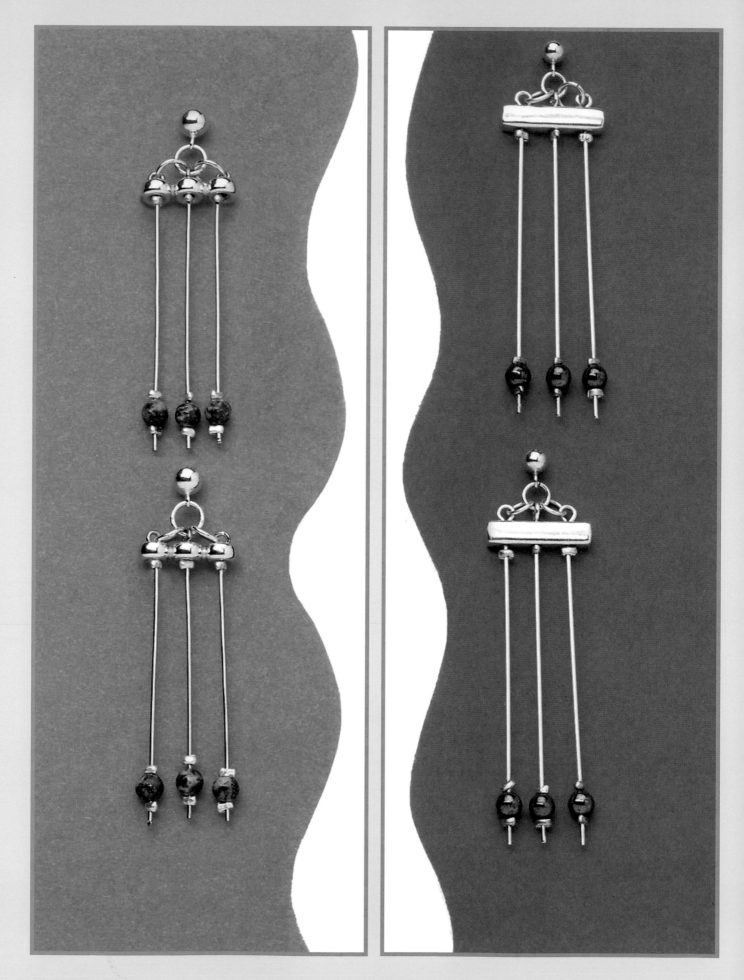

Dangling trio

Convert spacer bars and head pins into a swinging set of earrings

by Cynthia Williams

Bold and basic with an eye-catching appeal . . . these earrings convey a striking message with their elongated lines, pendulum-like sway, and flicker of color. Don't limit yourself to this symmetrical pattern. Be daring and vary the length of the head pins. Add sparkle. Combine gold and silver. Have fun. No matter what the approach, compliments will swing your way.

SupplyList

- **6** 4mm round beads
- **2** three-hole spacer beads, approx. 16mm
- **6** 2½-in. (6.4cm) head pins or eye pins
- **18** round crimp beads
- **6** 5mm jump rings
- pair of 4mm ball post earrings
- chainnose pliers
- roundnose pliers
- diagonal wire cutters

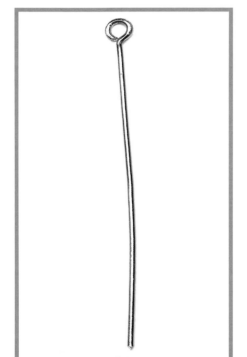

1 If you are using eye pins, skip to step 2. To make an eye pin, trim the head off of a head pin and make a plain loop at one end (see Basic Techniques, p. 6). Repeat with the remaining head pins.

2 Insert an eye pin into each opening of a three-hole spacer. String a crimp bead onto each eye pin directly beneath the spacer. Flatten each crimp with chainnose pliers (Basic Techniques). String a second crimp bead onto each eye pin ⅜ in. (10mm) from the end and flatten the crimps. String a 4mm round bead and a crimp bead onto each eye pin, flattening the crimps as you go.

3 Open a jump ring (Basic Techniques) and link it through the eye pin on the left side. Close the jump ring. Repeat with a jump ring on the right side. Open a third jump ring and slide it through one of the closed jump rings, the center eye pin, and the remaining closed jump ring.

4 Slide an earring post's loop on the open jump ring and close the jump ring. Make a second earring to match the first.

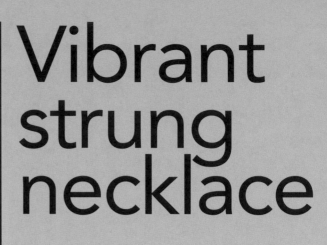

Vibrant strung necklace

A dichroic glass pendant sets off a vibrant arrangement of stones and glass beads

by Naomi Fujimoto

Since this necklace lacks a fixed supply list or stringing pattern, it may seem like a daunting task to make one. However, it's easy with some loose guidelines for creating a necklace of random beads: First, don't feel limited by the supply list when selecting beads. The list is intended only for illustrative purposes. Second, select different colors, materials, and shapes, but use beads of approximately the same diameter. Third, select a pendant after you've made part of the necklace (you'll have a better idea of what colors to highlight). Although it's conventional to start with the pendant as the focal point, selecting the pendant first might limit the range of colors in the strands. Finally, check the length of your necklace numerous times to ensure a perfect fit.

1 **necklace** • Determine the finished length of your necklace. (The top strand of this necklace measures 16 in./41cm; the bottom strand is ½ in./1.3cm longer.) Add 6 in. (15cm) and cut two pieces of beading wire to that length.

1b Center the pendant on one strand. String enough cylinder beads to fill the pendant's bail (its hanging loop). These small beads prevent other beads from sliding into the bail.

2 For the upper strand, string approximately 7 in. (18cm) of assorted beads and spacers on each end. Choose colors and shapes that look good next to each other. Tape the ends. Allow 1½ in. (3.8cm) for the clasp when determining where to stop stringing.

SupplyList

necklace
- pendant (dichroic glass, Eclectica, 262-641-0910)
- 4–5mm gemstone buttons and chips (amethyst, aquamarine, carnelian, citrine, coral, garnet, iolite, peridot)
- 4mm Swarovski crystals, bicone and round
- 3–4mm Czech fire-polished beads
- **12** 2.5 or 3mm round silver beads
- **20–30** Delica beads
- 4mm silver spacers
- flexible beading wire, .014 or .015
- **4** crimp beads
- two-strand clasp (Saki Silver, 513-861-9626)
- chainnose or crimping pliers
- diagonal wire cutters

earrings
- leftover beads and spacers
- 2 2-in. (5cm) head pins
- pair of earring wires
- chainnose pliers
- roundnose pliers
- diagonal wire cutters

3a String the remaining strand of beading wire through the pendant below the first strand. String cylinder beads to fill the pendant's bail as in step 1b. String this strand about ¼ in. (6mm) longer on each end than the first strand. Tape the ends.

3b Check the finished length of the necklace. Remove the tape and add or remove beads, if necessary.

4 Working at one end of the necklace, string two round silver beads, a crimp bead, a round bead, and one half of the clasp on each strand. Go back through the last few beads strung and tighten each wire.

5 Repeat step 4 with the remaining pair of wires and the clasp half. Double check the length and add or remove beads as needed. Crimp the crimp beads (see Basic Techniques, p. 6), and trim the excess wire.

1 **earrings** • Select matching pairs of assorted gemstones, crystals, and spacers. String a head pin with beads as desired. Make the first half of a wrapped loop (Basic Techniques) above the beads.

2 Complete the wraps and attach the component to an earring wire. Make a second earring to match the first.

Long lariat

Vivid colors and beautiful materials provide instant style

by Dorothy Roberts McEwen

Simple to string but versatile in style, this lariat makes a fashionable addition to any jewelry collection. Wear it choker length, and the tails will stream to your waist. Or, shift the focus down a few inches and loosely tie the ends to fill in an open neckline. Be daring and wear it in reverse — you'll have the perfect trailing detail for a V-backed dress.

1 Cut two 65-in. (1.7m) pieces of beading wire. String approximately 30 size 11º seed beads over both wires. Center the beads on the wires.

SupplyList

- 20mm (approx.) large-hole focal bead
- **50–60** 4–8mm accent beads, assorted shapes
- **10–20** 4mm round crystals, color matching accent beads
- **10–15** 4mm bicone crystals, color matching seed beads
- **7–10g** seed beads, size 8º
- **7–10g** seed beads, size 11º
- flexible beading wire, .014 or .015
- **5** crimp beads
- crimping pliers
- diagonal wire cutters

2 String a crimp bead over all four wires. Pull the ends to form a loop. Check the size of the loop to be sure the accent beads fit through. Add or remove beads, if necessary. Crimp the bead with crimping pliers to make a folded crimp (see Basic Techniques, p. 6).

3 String the focal bead over the four strands, covering the folded crimp.

4 Separate the wires and begin stringing seed beads and accent beads, staggering the placement of similar beads from strand to strand. Bead each strand until it is within 2 in. (5cm) of the desired length. (These strands extend 29½ in./75cm beyond the focal bead.) If desired, vary the lengths of the strands.

5 String a crimp bead, 6–10 seed beads, an accent bead, and a seed bead. Repeat on the remaining three strands.

6 a Go back through the accent bead, the seed beads, the crimp bead, and a few more seed beads. Repeat on the remaining three strands.

6 b Tighten the wires and check the fit. Add or remove beads, if necessary. Crimp the crimp bead on each strand and trim the excess wire.

Grand strands

Gemstones in four shapes and colors unite in a bold multistrand necklace

by Diana Grossman

You'll cover all the bases in one striking necklace by mixing gemstone shapes, sizes, and colors. Select the most unusual shape first, then more common shapes; different gemstones are not always available in the same cuts. Keep the sizes within a couple of millimeters of the first shape chosen to make the necklace well-balanced. Finally, choose a pendant in proportion with the gemstones' sizes. Follow these basic guidelines to score a colorful and captivating accessory.

SupplyList

- pendant, top drilled
- 4 16-in. (41cm) strands 4–10mm gemstones, four shapes and colors
- 16–18 3mm or 4mm faceted round Czech beads
- 16 or more 3mm round spacers
- flexible beading wire, .014 or .015
- Fireline fishing line, 6-lb. test
- 8 crimp beads
- 7mm jump ring (optional)
- four-strand clasp
- beading needle, #10
- G-S Hypo Cement
- chainnose pliers
- roundnose pliers
- diagonal wire cutters

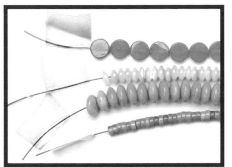

1a Determine the finished length of your necklace. (The jewel-toned necklace is 16 in./41cm; the pastel 18 in./46cm.) Add 6 in. (15cm) and cut four pieces of beading wire to that length.

1b Tape one end of each wire. Transfer beads from their temporary stringing material to beading wire until the necklace is within 1 in. (2.5cm) of the desired length.

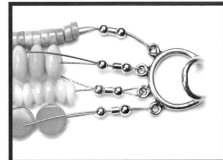

2 On one end of each wire, string a 3mm round spacer, a crimp bead, a spacer, and the respective loop on half the clasp. Go back through the beads just strung and tighten the wire. Remove the tape and repeat on the other end. Check the fit. If necessary, add 3mm round spacers to lengthen or remove gemstones to shorten. Crimp the crimp beads (see Basic Techniques, p. 6), and trim the excess wire.

3 Open a jump ring (Basic Techniques) and string it through the pendant's loop. Close the jump ring.

4 Thread a beading needle with a 7-in. (18cm) piece of Fireline. String approximately 2.5 in. (6.4cm) of 3mm or 4mm beads, the pendant, and 2.5 in. of 3mm or 4mm beads.

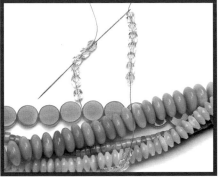

5 Encircle the necklace with the beaded Fireline. Go back through all the beads, exiting from the last bead strung. To make the pendant detachable, string enough beads on the Fireline to maneuver over the strands and clasp.

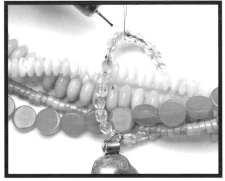

6 Tie the ends in a surgeon's knot (Basic Techniques). Trim the Fireline to 1/8 in. (3mm) and apply glue to the knot. Gently maneuver the knot inside an adjacent bead.

Shimmering crystals

Faceted crystals lend motion to this cool, shimmering bracelet and earrings

by Molli Schultz

Any monochromatic scheme will sparkle; try sherbety orange combined with muted pinks and peaches, or pale green with soft teals and aquas. The shimmering finishes and substantial width are ideal for a gal on the go, or for someone just watching the world go by.

1 **bracelet** • For each dangle, open a 3mm jump ring (see Basic Techniques, p. 6) and string a saucer and a closed 2mm jump ring. Close the jump ring. Make a total of 25 dangles. Set one aside for the chain extender in step 6.

2 Determine the finished length of your bracelet, add 5 in. (13cm), and cut five pieces of beading wire to that length. On each wire, center 10–12 4mm fire-polished beads interspersed with one or two dangles. String the lightest colored fire-polished beads on the outside strands, the darkest on the second and fourth strands, and the remaining beads on the middle strand.

Supply List

bracelet
- **25–28** 6mm or 9mm crystal saucers, top drilled
- **5** 8-in. (20cm) strands 4mm Czech fire-polished beads, **2** strands each of two colors and **1** strand of a third color
- **2** five-strand spacer bars
- **20** 3mm round spacer beads
- **2** five-to-one connector bars
- flexible beading wire, .014 or .015
- **27–30** 3mm jump rings
- **25–28** 2mm jump rings
- **10** crimp beads
- lobster claw clasp
- 1½–2 in. (3.8–5cm) chain, 5mm links
- chainnose and roundnose pliers or **2** pairs of chainnose pliers
- diagonal wire cutters
- crimping pliers (optional)

earrings
- **2** 6mm or 9mm crystal saucers, top drilled (Eclectica)
- **18** 4mm Czech fire-polished beads, **8** each of two colors and **2** of the third color, left over from the bracelet
- **2** five-to-one connector bars
- **2** 3mm jump rings
- **8** 1½-in. decorative head pins
- **15** in. (38cm) 1.5mm fine chain
- pair of decorative earring wires
- chainnose pliers
- roundnose pliers
- diagonal wire cutters

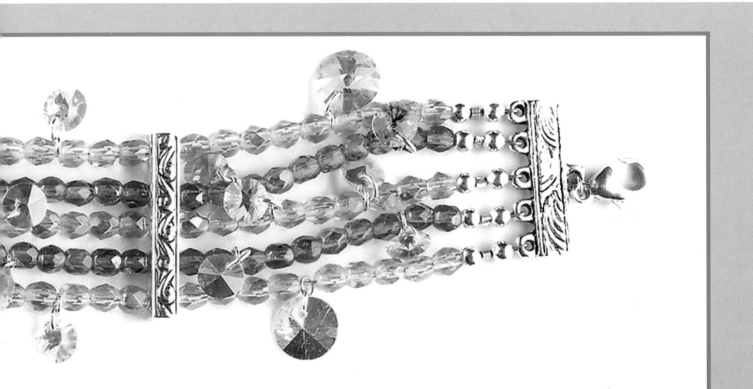

3 On each end of each wire, string the respective hole of a spacer bar. String crystals and dangles as in step 2, until the bracelet is within 2 in. (5cm) of the finished length.

4 On each end of each wire, string a round spacer, a crimp bead, a round spacer, and the respective loop of a clasp half. Go back through the beads just strung and tighten the wires. Check the fit, and add or remove beads from each end if necessary. Crimp the crimp beads (Basic Techniques) and trim the excess wire.

1a earrings • Cut five pieces of chain: one 2¾, two 2¼, and two 2 in. (7, 5.7, and 5cm, respectively).

1b Open a 3mm jump ring and string a saucer and an end link of the longest chain. Close the jump ring.

5 Open a 3mm jump ring. Connect the lobster claw clasp to the remaining loop of the connector bar with the jump ring. Close the jump ring.

6 Open a 3mm jump ring. Connect an end link of chain to the other connector bar's remaining loop. Close the jump ring. Open the extra dangle's 3mm jump ring and attach it to the other end link of chain. Close the jump ring.

2 String a fire-polished bead on a 1½-in. (3.8cm) decorative head pin and make a plain loop (Basic Techniques) above the bead. (Set aside the remaining part of the head pin's wire for step 4.) String a total of four dangles in two colors.

3 Open the loop of a dangle and string an end link of chain. Close the loop. Repeat with each of the three remaining dangles and chain pieces, matching crystal colors on the chains.

4 String a crystal on a wire (from step 2). Make a plain loop at each end. Make a total of four dangles in the two colors used in step 2. Trim the head from a head pin and make a fifth dangle with the third-color crystal.

5 Open the loop of the fifth crystal dangle and string the remaining end link of the longest chain. Close the loop. Repeat with each of the remaining dangles and chain pieces, matching crystal colors with chain lengths.

6a Open the loop above the crystal on the longest chain and string the center loop of the connector bar. Close the loop. Repeat with each of the remaining chain pieces, attaching the shortest lengths of chain to the outer loops of the connector bar.

6b Open the loop on an earring wire and string the remaining loop of the connector bar. Close the loop. Make a second earring to match the first.

EDITOR'S TIP
You may use 3mm, 4mm, 5mm, or 6mm Czech fire-polished beads, but use a consistent size throughout the bracelet. Mixing sizes will result in uneven strand lengths.

Lapis lazuli bracelet and earrings

Vibrant blue and silver combine in a gorgeous bracelet and earrings set

by Karin Buckingham

This seemingly random but nicely balanced bracelet satisfies yearnings for both harmonious equilibrium and creative expression. Stringing the individual patterns in each strand brings balance; wrapping the strands into one bracelet is the creative flourish.

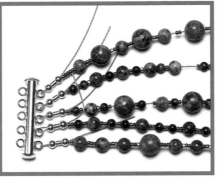

1 **bracelet** • Determine the finished length of your bracelet, add 5 in. (13cm), and cut five pieces of wire to that length. String patterns of gemstones and seed beads on each wire until you are within 1 in. (2.5cm) of your desired length. (Two of these strands use larger beads, one uses all three sizes, and two strands use smaller beads.)

2 On both ends of each strand, string a 3mm round spacer, a crimp bead, a spacer, and half the clasp. (Be sure each clasp half is positioned correctly.) Go back through the last beads strung, tighten the wires, and check the fit. Add or remove beads, if necessary. Crimp the crimp beads (see Basic Techniques, p. 6) and trim the excess wire.

SupplyList

bracelet
- 16-in. (41cm) strand 8mm round, lapis lazuli
- 16-in. strand 5mm round, lapis
- 16-in. strand 3mm round, lapis
- 2g size 14º faceted seed beads
- **24** 3mm round spacer beads
- flexible beading wire, .014 or .015
- **12** crimp beads
- five-strand slide clasp
- chainnose or crimping pliers
- diagonal wire cutters

earrings
- **2** 8mm round, lapis
- **2** 5mm round, lapis
- **6** 3mm round, lapis
- **8** size 14º faceted seed beads
- **6** 2-in. (5cm) head pins
- pair of earring wires
- chainnose pliers
- roundnose pliers
- diagonal wire cutters

3 Cut a piece of wire 2 in. (5cm) longer than the wires in step 1. String 3mm rounds and seed beads as desired until the strand is 2 in. longer than the other finished strands. On one end, string a 3mm spacer, a crimp bead, a spacer, and the top loop of a clasp half. Go back through the last beads strung and crimp the crimp bead. Trim the excess wire.

4 Loosely wrap this strand in a spiral around the other strands. Check the length, making sure it reaches the bottom loop of the remaining clasp half. Add or remove beads as needed. String a spacer, a crimp bead, a spacer, and the bottom clasp loop. Go back through the last beads strung, tighten the wire, and crimp the crimp bead. Trim the excess wire.

1 **earrings** • String a 3mm round and a seed bead onto a head pin. Trim the head pin ⅜ in. (10mm) above the top bead and make a plain loop (Basic Techniques). Make three bead units. Reserve one of the trimmed wire pieces.

2 Make a plain loop at one end of the reserved wire. Open the loop, string the three bead units on the loop, and close the loop.

3 String an 8mm round, a seed bead, and a 5mm round on the wire.

4 Make a plain loop above the top bead. Open the loop of an earring wire and attach the earring. Close the loop. Make a second earring to match the first.

Sparkling blue crystals

Compose a dazzling, double-strand necklace, bracelet, and earrings set

by Lynne Dixon-Speller

The sapphire-blue hues of these sparkling crystals beg to be used in a monochromatic necklace. The variety of shapes and sizes adds visual interest to the design, while the deep, vibrant blue ties it all together in this gorgeous jewelry set.

SupplyList

necklace
- **11** 10mm round crystals
- **90** 6mm round crystals
- **12** 8mm cube-shaped crystals
- **22** 6mm cube-shaped crystals
- **8** 3mm round beads
- flexible beading wire, .014 or .015
- **4** crimp beads
- two-strand toggle clasp
- chainnose or crimping pliers
- diagonal wire cutters

bracelet
- **5** 10mm round crystals
- **37** 6mm round crystals
- **4** 8mm cube-shaped crystals
- **9** 6mm cube-shaped crystals
- **8** 3mm round beads
- flexible beading wire, .014 or .015
- **4** crimp beads
- two-strand toggle clasp
- chainnose or crimping pliers
- diagonal wire cutters

earrings
- **2** 10mm round crystals
- **2** 6mm round crystals
- **2** 8mm cube-shaped crystals
- **2** 6mm cube-shaped crystals
- **32** 3mm bicone crystals
- 8 in. (20cm) 20-gauge wire
- **4** 2-in. (5cm) head pins
- **2** 4mm jump rings
- pair leverback earring wires
- roundnose pliers
- chainnose pliers
- diagonal wire cutters

1 **necklace •** Determine the finished length of your necklace's inner strand (this one is 17½ in./44.5cm) and add 6 in. (15cm). Cut one piece of beading wire to that length and one 1 in. (2.5cm) longer. On the longer strand, string a 6mm round crystal, 3mm bead, crimp bead, and 3mm. Go through the clasp's lower loop and back through the beads. Tighten the wire and crimp the crimp bead (see Basic Techniques, p. 6). Trim the excess wire.

2 String a 10mm round crystal to begin the pattern shown. Repeat until the strand is the desired length. (The last repeat may not be a complete pattern.)

3 String a 3mm bead, a crimp bead, and a 3mm bead and go through the lower loop of the remaining clasp section. Go back through the last three beads, tighten the wire, and crimp the crimp bead. Trim the excess wire.

4 On the remaining strand, string two 6mm crystals, a 3mm bead, crimp bead, and 3mm bead and go through the clasp's upper loop. Go back through the last three beads, tighten the wire, and crimp the crimp bead. Trim the excess wire.

5 String an 8mm crystal cube to begin the pattern shown. Repeat until this strand is approximately 1 in. (2.5cm) shorter than the first strand. Finish the end as in step 3, but go through the clasp's upper loop.

1 earrings • Open a jump ring (Basic Techniques) and attach it to the earring loop.

2 Cut two 2-in. (5cm) lengths of wire. Make a loop (Basic Techniques) at one end of each wire. String ten 3mm bicones on one wire. Trim the wire to 3/8 in. (1cm) and make a loop above the end bicone. Make a second dangle with six bicones.

3 On one head pin, string a 6mm and a 10mm round crystal. On another, string a 6mm and an 8mm cube. Trim the wires to 3/8 in. and turn a loop above the crystal on each dangle.

4 Open the loops on the head pins and attach them to the beaded wires as shown. Close the loops.

5 Attach both dangles to the open jump ring on the earring finding. Close the jump ring (Basic Techniques). Make a second earring to match the first.

1 **bracelet** • Determine the finished length of your bracelet, add 5 in. (13cm), and cut two pieces of beading wire to that length. String a crimp bead, a 3mm bead, and half the clasp. Go back through the beads. Tighten the wire and crimp the crimp bead.

2 String a 10mm round crystal over both the long wire and the tail. Trim the excess wire. Repeat the pattern shown above twice. Check the length and add or remove beads as necessary.

3 String a 3mm bead, crimp bead, 3mm bead, and the toggle. (The extra 3mm bead on this end lets the toggle pivot easily.) Go back through the last three beads. Tighten the wire and crimp the crimp bead. Trim the excess wire.

4 On the remaining wire, string a crimp bead, a 3mm bead, and the clasp. Go back through the beads, tighten the wire, and crimp the crimp bead. String the pattern shown above twice, covering the long wire and tail with the first few beads. Make the second strand the same length as the first.

5 Repeat step 3 to finish the bracelet.

Aquamarine jewelry set

Cool aquamarine and frosty quartz melt into a necklace that evokes a sense of warm days by the sea

by Karin Buckingham

Named Aqua Marina by the Romans because it reminded them of seawater, this lovely gemstone comes in several shades of translucent blue. Here, it's paired with translucent quartz, faceted silver seed beads, and whimsical X-shaped spacers to make an elegant salute to spring.

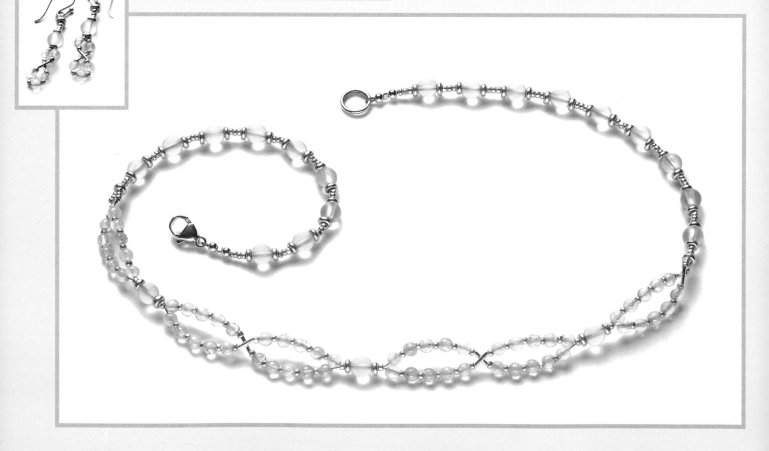

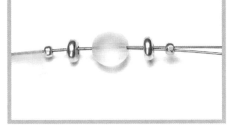

1 **necklace •** Determine the finished length of your necklace (This necklace is 18½ in./47cm), add 6 in. (15cm), and cut two pieces of beading wire to that length. Center a quartz bead on both strands. Add a disc and a seed bead on each side. Tape one side close to the seed bead so the beads remain centered.

2 Separate the strands, and string each with an alternating pattern of five aquamarines and five seed beads, starting with an aquamarine.

3 String an X-shaped spacer as shown.

4 String an alternating pattern of five seed beads and five aquamarines as in step 2, starting with a seed bead.

5a String a seed bead, a disc, a quartz bead, a disc, and a seed bead over both strands. Repeat steps 2 and 3.

5b Remove the tape and repeat steps 2 through 5a on the other side of the center beads.

6 String three seed beads on each strand. Over both strands, string one disc, three seed beads, one disc, and a quartz bead. Repeat the pattern nine times. Repeat step 6 on the other end.

7 Check the fit and add or remove beads from each end, if necessary. String a round, a crimp bead, a round, and a clasp over both wires. Go back through the last beads strung. Tighten the wire, crimp the crimp bead (see Basic Techniques, p. 6), and trim the excess wire. Repeat on the other end, using a soldered jump ring or a split ring in place of the clasp.

Supply List

all projects
- chainnose pliers
- diagonal wire cutters
- crimping pliers (optional)

necklace
- 16-in. (41cm) strand 4mm round beads, aquamarine
- 16-in. strand 6mm round beads, frosted quartz
- 1g faceted seed beads, size 11º
- 4 4.1mm X-shaped spacers, (Rio Grande, 800-545-6566, riogrande.com)
- 44 or more 4mm disc-shaped spacers
- 4 3mm round spacer beads
- flexible beading wire, .014 or .015
- soldered jump ring or split ring
- 2 crimp beads
- lobster claw clasp

bracelet
- 20 4mm aquamarine beads
- 7 6mm frosted quartz beads
- 2 4.1mm X-shaped spacers
- 16 4mm silver disc-shaped spacers
- 1g faceted seed beads, size 11º
- 4 3mm silver round spacer beads
- flexible beading wire, .014 or .015
- 2 crimp beads
- lobster claw clasp and soldered or split ring

earrings
- 10 4 mm round aquamarine beads
- 2 6mm frosted quartz beads
- 2 4.1mm X-shaped spacers (Rio Grande)
- 6 4mm silver disc-shaped spacers
- 22 faceted seed beads, size 11º
- flexible beading wire, .014 or .015
- 2 crimp beads
- 2 4mm soldered jump rings
- pair earring wires

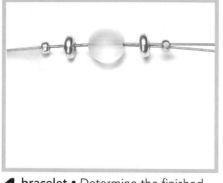

1 **bracelet** • Determine the finished length of your bracelet and add 5 in. (13cm). Cut two pieces of beading wire to this length. Center a quartz bead on both strands. Add a disc and a seed bead on each side.

2 On each side of the center beads, separate the strands and string an aquamarine and a seed bead. Repeat a total of four times on each strand.

3 On each side, string an X-shaped spacer as shown.

4 String three seed beads on each strand. Over both strands, string one disc, three seed beads, a disc, and a quartz bead. Repeat twice. Repeat on the other side.

5 Check the fit and add or remove beads, if necessary. String a 3mm round spacer bead, a crimp bead, a 3mm round, and the clasp over both wires. Go back through the last beads strung, tighten the wire, crimp the crimp bead, and trim the excess wires. Repeat on the other end, using a soldered jump ring or a split ring in place of the clasp.

1 **earrings** • Cut a 5 in. (13cm) piece of beading wire. Alternate seed beads and aquamarine beads three times, beginning and ending with a seed bead. Center the beads on the wire.

2 String an X-shaped spacer, leading each strand through half the X. String a seed bead, an aquamarine, and a seed bead on each wire. Then string a disc, a quartz bead, a disc, three seed beads, and a disc over both wires.

3a Pull the wires tight to align them. String a crimp bead and a 4mm soldered jump ring. Go back through the crimp bead and the disc. Tighten the wire, crimp the crimp bead, and trim the excess wire. Open the earring wire loop, and attach the jump ring. Close the loop.

3b Make a second earring to match the first.

WIREWORK

Elevate the quality of your jewelry-making by mastering a few basic wireworking techniques. Practice making loops and spirals with soft craft wire before graduating to sterling silver or gold-filled wire. Attention to detail – making round loops that are the same size, keeping wraps tight and even – will pay off with professional-looking jewelry.

Gemstone links

Use an easy wire technique to connect gemstone nuggets

by Lea Rose Nowicki

This fast necklace is an excellent way to get started working with wire, and the results look undeniably professional, even for a first-timer. Practice your loops with inexpensive copper wire from a hardware or craft store. When you can turn a round loop, buy sterling silver, nickel silver, or gold-filled wire — all are good choices for jewelry-making. Choose chunky beads in your favorite color, then find a clasp with a narrow tip that will easily hook onto a wire loop.

1 String a nugget on the end of the wire. Bend the wire at a right angle about ⅜ in. (1cm) from the tip.

2 Turn a plain loop (see Basic Techniques, p. 6) above the nugget. Trim the wire below the nugget to ⅜ in.

SupplyList

- 16-in. (41cm) strand 2–2.5cm gemstone nuggets, chrysoprase (above), faceted citrine (below)
- 3mm flat spacer bead
- 3 ft. (.9m) 20-gauge wire
- 2-in. (5cm) head pin
- S-hook or hook clasp
- chainnose pliers
- roundnose pliers
- diagonal wire cutters

WIREWORK

3a Turn another loop below the nugget.

3b Prepare enough nuggets to fit comfortably around your neck. Make one loop on one nugget large enough to accommodate the hook of the clasp. (You'll use this nugget on the end opposite the clasp.) Set aside one stone for the dangle.

4 Open a loop (Basic Techniques) on one nugget and attach it to the loop on another. Close the loop. Connect the remaining nuggets in the same way. Attach the nugget with one larger loop to either end of the necklace using its smaller loop.

5 Open the loop on the nugget at the opposite end of the necklace and attach the clasp. Close the loop.

6 To make the dangle, string a 3mm flat spacer and the reserved nugget on a head pin. Trim the wire to ⅜ in. and make a loop above the bead.

7 Open the large loop on the end without the clasp and attach the dangle.

8 To wear the necklace, connect the clasp to the large loop.

Pearl dangles

Cluster round pearls and faceted beads on a chain necklace, bracelet, and earrings

by Naomi Fujimoto

The secret to this cascade of bubbly baubles? Each bead is larger than its corresponding chain link, so attaching one per link crowds and spills them playfully around your neck. For a necklace or bracelet, select a chain strong enough to support 40 or 50 beads. And don't be afraid to use dyed or man-made beads – faux can be fabulous.

1 **necklace** • String a 12mm bead on a head pin. Make a plain loop (see Basic Techniques, p. 6) above the bead. Make a total of 35–50 dangles with various beads.

2 Determine the finished length of your necklace. (This one is 18 in./46cm.) Cut a piece of chain to that length. Open a 5mm jump ring (Basic Techniques) and attach the center dangle to the chain's center link. Close the jump ring.

3 Open the loop on a 12mm dangle and attach it to a link next to the center dangle. Attach another 12mm dangle to the next link. Repeat on the other side of the center dangle.

4 Attach one dangle per chain link, covering approximately 6 in. (15cm) of the chain. On each side of this necklace there are: an 8mm crystal, two 12mm pearls, a 12mm crystal, a 10mm teardrop pearl, a 10mm round pearl, an 8mm crystal, a 12mm pearl, an 8mm round pearl, a 10mm crystal, a 12mm pearl, an 8mm crystal, a 12mm pearl, an 8mm round pearl, and an 8mm oval pearl.

5 Check the fit, allowing 1 in. (2.5cm) for finishing. Trim an equal number of links from each end of the chain, if necessary. On each end, use a jump ring to attach half of the clasp.

SupplyList

all projects
• chainnose pliers
• roundnose pliers
• diagonal wire cutters

necklace
• **17 or more** 12mm round beads, **2** each in eight colors, plus **1** for the center (16 in./41cm pearl strands, Eclectica, 262-641-0910)
• **4 or more** 10mm round beads, **2** each in two colors
• **10 or more** 8mm round beads, **2** each in five colors
• **4 or more** 8–10mm teardrop or oval pearls, **2** each in two colors
• 18–23 in. (46–58cm) chain, 4–5mm links
• **35–50** 1-in. (2.5cm) 22-gauge head pins
• **3** 5mm jump rings
• toggle clasp

bracelet
• **18 or more** 12mm round beads, **2** each in nine colors
• **4 or more** 10mm round beads, **2** each in two colors
• **10 or more** 8mm round beads, **2** each in five colors
• **5 or more** 8–10mm teardrop or potato pearls, **2** each in two colors, plus **1** for the extender's dangle
• 6½–8 in. (16.5–20cm) chain, 4–5mm links
• **35–50** 1-in. (2.5cm) 22-gauge head pins
• **2** 5mm jump rings
• lobster claw clasp
• 1-in. (2.5cm) chain extender

earrings
• **2** 12mm round beads
• **2** 10mm round beads
• **2** 8mm beads
• **2** in. (5cm) chain, 4–5mm links
• **6** 1-in. (2.5cm) 22-gauge head pins
• pair of earring wires

1 **bracelet •** Determine the finished length of your bracelet and cut a piece of chain to that length. Make 35–50 dangles as in step 1 of the necklace. Starting at one end of the chain, attach one dangle per link until the bracelet is within 1 in. (2.5cm) of the desired length. (Repeat the necklace pattern, omitting the center jump ring unit.)

2 Check the fit, and trim chain links if necessary. Open a jump ring and attach one end of the bracelet and one end of a 1-in. (2.5cm) chain extender. Close the jump ring. Open a dangle's loop and attach it to the end of the extender. Close the loop. Attach the clasp to the other end of the bracelet with a jump ring.

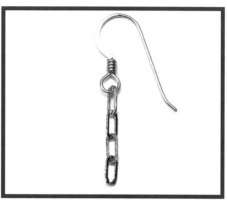

1 **earrings •** Cut a four-link piece of chain. Open the loop on an earring wire and attach the chain. Close the loop.

2 Make an 8mm, a 10mm, and a 12mm dangle as in step 1 of the necklace. Open the 10mm dangle's loop and attach it to the second chain link. Close the loop. Attach the 12mm and 8mm dangles on the third and fourth links, respectively. Make a second earring to match the first.

DESIGN GUIDELINES
• The largest bead size forms the majority of the beaded section in the necklace or bracelet. Change the scale by including fewer 12mm beads, or by substituting smaller beads with a delicate chain.
• Plan on 35–50 dangles to make a 6-in. (15cm) beaded section. The total number of beads is dependent on the size of the chain's links.
• For the necklace, attach the dangles in a symmetrical pattern to reduce your work in selecting and arranging beads.
• Consider substituting squares or ovals for the round beads (unusual shapes are available in limited sizes and colors).
• For a tapered effect, attach smaller beads near the ends, rather than at the center of the necklace's beaded section.

Dichroic links bracelet

by Irina Miech

Wrapped loops connect dichroic glass squares and crystals in a contemporary bracelet

Encased in sterling silver, brilliant dichroic glass squares stand out when linked with geometrically contrasting oval crystals. In addition, the crystals highlight colorful flecks in the multihued glass. A stylish clasp puts the final touch on a stunning bracelet.

SupplyList

- **4 or 5** 12mm dichroic glass window components
- **5** 9 x 6mm oval crystals
- 15 in. (38cm) 22- or 24-gauge sterling silver wire, half hard
- 5–6mm silver split ring (optional)
- silver toggle clasp
- chainnose pliers
- roundnose pliers
- diagonal wire cutters
- split-ring pliers (optional)

1 Cut a 3-in. (7.6cm) piece of wire. String an oval bead and make the first half of a wrapped loop (see Basic Techniques, p. 6) at each end. Make a total of five bead units.

2 Attach one bead unit's loop to half the clasp. Attach the other loop to a dichroic component. Complete the wraps. Continue attaching bead units and components in an alternating pattern. Do not complete the wraps on the last bead unit.

3 Attach the last bead unit's loop to the remaining clasp half and complete the wraps. If the bracelet's last link is a dichroic component, attach the remaining clasp half with a split ring.

Seductive swirls

Create gorgeous curves with wire and glass dangles

by Wendy Witchner

A few simple twists with your pliers will transform wire into sexy earrings. Cut glass or gemstone dangles swing saucily below the earrings' graceful curves, flashing a spark of color.

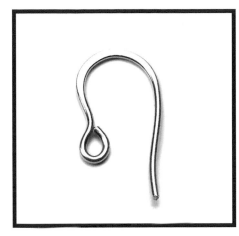

earring wires • Cut a 1½-in. (3.8cm) piece of wire. At one end, make a plain loop (see Basic Techniques, p. 6). Bend the wire ⅛ in. (3mm) above the loop. Using your fingers and chainnose pliers, curve the wire into a question-mark shape. Hammer each side. Trim the excess wire and file the end. Repeat to make a second earring wire.

Supply**List**

Supply List
• **2 preset Swarovski channels** (Rio Grande, 800-545-6566, riogrande.com)
• **2 2–2.5mm round beads**
• **11 in. (28cm) 20-gauge round wire, half hard**
• pair of earring wires or 3 in. (7.6cm) 20-gauge round wire, half hard
• chainnose pliers
• roundnose pliers
• diagonal wire cutters
• ball-peen hammer
• bench block or anvil
• metal file or emery board

WIREWORK

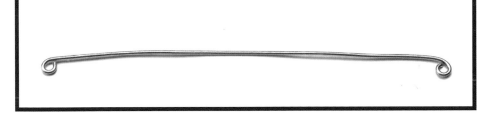

1 **earrings** • Cut a 3½-in. (9cm) piece of wire. File the ends. With roundnose pliers, make a small loop at each end of the wire. The loops should curve toward each other.

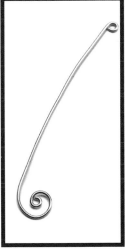

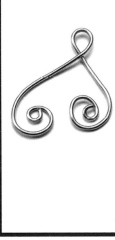

2 Position the chainnose pliers across one loop to hold it in place. Using your fingers, coil one end of the wire to form a spiral, making almost one full rotation around the small loop.

3 Repeat step 2 on the other end of the wire. To make the top loop, twist a loop in the wire just off-center. The spirals should be at different heights, both facing inward. If desired, hammer the shape several times on each side.

4 For the dangle, cut a 1¼-in. (3.2cm) piece of wire. File both ends. With your roundnose pliers, make a small plain loop (Basic Techniques) at one end. String a round bead on the wire and make a large plain loop at the other end.

5 Open the small loop on the dangle. String the channel on the small loop and close the loop. Open the dangle's large loop and attach it to the shape's top loop. Close the loop.

6 Open the loop on an earring wire and attach it to the shape's top loop. Close the loop. Make a second earring the mirror image of the first.

Shapely spirals

Make lively coiled wire earrings

by Lea Rose Nowicki

Create sophisticated spiral earrings by coiling wire around a pen and hanging an accent bead at one end. Experiment with the type of wire (such as square or twisted), the number and spacing of the wraps, or the size of the pen to create a variety of coils. Let your creativity spiral out of control to put your own twist on these stylish earrings.

Supply List

- 2 4–8mm accent beads
- 12–18 in. (30-46cm) 20- or 22-gauge wire, half hard
- 2 1-in. (2.5cm) head pins
- pair of earring wires
- chainnose pliers
- roundnose pliers
- diagonal wire cutters
- pen with a graduated barrel

WIREWORK

1 Determine the length of each finished coil, multiply by four, and cut two pieces of wire to that length. (For example, cut a 6-in./15cm piece of wire to make a coil 1½ in/3.8cm in length.) Wrap the wire tightly around the pen barrel. Remove the wire coil.

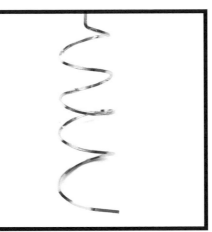

2 If desired, adjust the coil's shape with your fingers. Bend ⅜ in. (1cm) of the wire upward at a right angle.

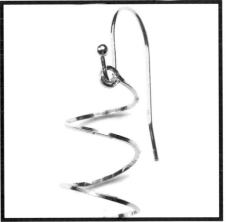

3 Make a plain loop (see Basic Techniques, p. 6) at the top end of the coil. If necessary, trim excess wire at the bottom of the coil, allowing ⅜ in. for a plain loop. Make a plain loop.

4 String an accent bead on a head pin. Make a plain loop above the bead.

5 Open the loop on the dangle and attach it to the coil's bottom loop. Close the dangle's loop.

6 Open an earring wire and attach the coil's top loop. Close the earring wire. Make a second earring the mirror image of the first (to make the coil, twist the wire in the opposite direction from the first coil).

Metal washer collection

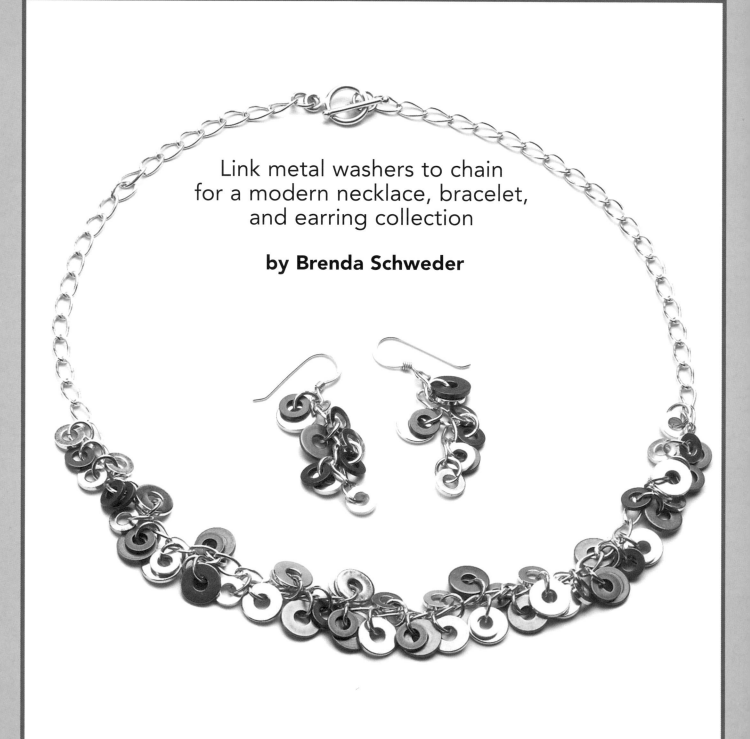

Link metal washers to chain
for a modern necklace, bracelet,
and earring collection

by Brenda Schweder

This nifty jewelry set emphasizes the open design of everyday metal washers. The necklace, bracelet, and earrings require only two sizes and two colors of washers, and the technique is equally manageable – attach the washers to chain with jump rings, add a clasp, and go!

SupplyList

all projects
- **2** pairs of chainnose pliers (or chainnose and roundnose pliers)
- diagonal wire cutters

necklace
- **15–20** 8mm silver washers
- **20–25** 6mm silver washers
- **15–20** 8mm brass washers
- **20–25** 6mm brass washers
- **2** ft. (.61m) silver chain, links at least 5mm
- **45–50** 5 or 6mm jump rings
- toggle clasp

bracelet
- **15–20** 8mm silver washers
- **20–25** 6mm silver washers
- **15–20** 8mm brass washers
- **20–25** 6mm brass washers
- **1** ft. (.3m) silver chain, links at least 5mm
- **45–50** 5 or 6mm jump rings
- toggle clasp

earrings
- **18–20** washers
- **2** pieces 1½-in. silver chain
- **10** 5 or 6mm jump rings
- pair of earring wires

1 **necklace** • Determine the finished length of your necklace (this one is 16 in./41cm), and cut a piece of chain to that length. Open a jump ring (see Basic Techniques, p. 6) and string on one or two washers.

2 Find the center link by folding the chain in half. Loop the jump ring through the center link of the chain and close it.

3 On each side of the center, use jump rings to attach one or two washers to subsequent chain links. (Make sure each dangle hangs downward from the chain.) Vary the colors and sizes, and include combinations of paired and single washers. Attach the washers to an equal number of links on each side of the center. (The washer section of this necklace extends 15 links on each side of the center.)

4 Check the fit. To shorten the necklace, cut equal numbers of links from each end. Use a jump ring to attach each half of a toggle clasp to an end link.

bracelet • Cut a segment of chain to fit comfortably around your wrist. Attach washers to each link of the chain as in the necklace. Finish the bracelet as in step 4.

1 **earrings** • Cut two five-link segments of chain. Open the loop on an earring wire and attach the end chain link.

1b Attach a pair of washers to the top link with a jump ring.

2 Continue adding washers to the remaining links. Make a second earring the mirror image of the first.

Simple and streamlined

Brilliant faceted briolettes shine in this simple, classy lariat

by Mindy Brooks

A pair of faceted beads and a length of rolo chain are the key elements in this modern lariat. Synthetic stones shine here, but the design adapts easily to dangling crystals, art beads, and authentic gemstones. Look for teardrop, pear-shaped, or elongated beads that keep the lariat's streamlined profile.

SupplyList

- **2** 25mm or **1** 25mm and **1** 18mm horizontally drilled teardrop briolettes
- 4 ft. (1.2m) rolo chain
- 5 in. (13cm) 20-gauge wire
- chainnose pliers
- roundnose pliers
- diagonal wire cutters

1 Center one briolette on a 2½-in. (6.4cm) length of wire and cross the wires above the bead.

2 Bend one of the wire ends so it points straight up above the bead.

3 Wrap the angled wire around the straight one, as if completing a wrapped loop (see Basic Techniques, p. 6). Trim the excess wrapping wire.

4 Use the straight wire to make the first half of a wrapped loop.

5 Slide the end link of chain into the loop.

6 Complete the wrapped loop and trim the excess wire. Repeat these steps to attach the remaining briolette to the other end of the chain.

Encased earrings

Coil wire around tube beads for an inventive pair of earrings

by Lilian Cartwright

Make these earrings to suit your style – create ornate dangles with multiple wraps, or go for a simpler look with just two or three coils. Try using art glass, gemstone, or even ceramic beads for a totally tubular look.

SupplyList

- **2** tube beads, up to 1½ in. (3.8cm) in length
- **2–6** 4–8mm spacers or rondelles
- **8–12 in.** (20–30cm) 22- or 24-gauge half-hard wire, gold-filled or sterling silver
- pair of earring wires
- chainnose pliers
- roundnose pliers
- diagonal wire cutters

1 Measure the length of a tube bead and multiply it by four. Cut a piece of wire to that length. Center a tube on the wire and bring one end (the wrapping wire) up over the bead.

2 Hold the wire at the bead's base and coil the wrapping wire snugly around the bead, encircling it at least twice.

3 Make a set of wraps (see Basic Techniques, p. 6) around the wire stem with the wrapping wire. Trim the excess wrapping wire.

4a String spacers or rondelles on the wire stem. Make a wrapped loop (Basic Techniques) above the top bead. Open the loop on an earring wire and attach the dangle. Close the loop.

4b Make a second earring the mirror image of the first.

Lush and leafy lariat

Glass and plastic merge along a line of copper

by Jane Konkel

Get a jump on falling leaves by mixing multicolored glass beads with plastic leaf-shaped beads – a splendid spin on today's trinket trend. Copper chain is the stalk's trellis, while wire veins and tendrils embellish each leaf. Combine unexpected colors inspired by the ever-changing foliage for an autumnal necklace and earrings set.

SupplyList

both projects
• chainnose pliers
• roundnose pliers
• diagonal wire cutters

necklace
• **10–15** glass or plastic leaf-shaped beads
• **10–15** 4mm bicone crystals
• 45 in. (1.1m) 20- or 22-gauge copper wire, or a combination of gauges
• 35–40 in. (.9–1m) copper curb chain (Rings & Things, 800-366-2156, rings-things.com)
• **13–18** 4mm copper jump rings
• copper toggle clasp (Rings & Things)

earrings
• **4** glass or plastic leaf-shaped beads
• **4** 4mm bicone crystals
• 12 in. (30cm) 20- or 22-gauge copper wire, or a combination of gauges
• 3 in. (7.6cm) copper curb chain (Rings & Things)
• **4** 4mm copper jump rings
• pair of niobium earring wires (Fire Mountain Gems, 800-355-2137, firemountaingems.com)

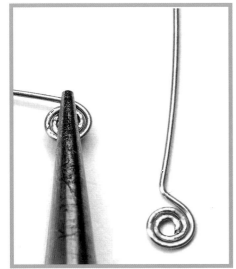

1 **necklace** • To make a wire spiral for a front-to-back–drilled bead, cut a 3-in. (7.6cm) piece of wire. Grasp the end of the wire with the tip of your roundnose pliers and form a small loop. After a complete turn, gently grasp the wire with chainnose pliers. Continue to form a spiral with your fingers until you have two or three coils.

2 String a crystal on the wire. Using the tip of your roundnose pliers, form a zig-zag pattern approximately ¼ in. (6mm) above the crystal. Bend the top of the wire up.

3 Using the largest part of your roundnose pliers, make the first half of a wrapped loop (see Basic Techniques, p. 6) perpendicular to the spiral, approximately ½ in. (1.3cm) above the last zig-zag.

4 String a leaf bead on the loop and complete the wraps. Repeat steps 1–4 for the remaining front-to-back–drilled beads.

5 To make a wire spiral for a side-to-side–drilled bead, follow step 1. Bend the top of the wire up. String a crystal on the wire. Place the largest part of your roundnose pliers approximately 1½ in. (3.8cm) from the end of the wire. Make the first half of a wrapped loop in the same plane as the spiral.

6 String a leaf bead on the wire and complete the wraps. Repeat steps 5 and 6 for the remaining side-to-side–drilled beads.

7 Determine the finished length of the lariat's choker. (This one is 15 in./38cm.) Double the measurement and cut a piece of chain to that length. Open a jump ring (Basic Techniques) and attach both ends of chain and the toggle half of the clasp. Close the jump ring. Attach another jump ring, the doubled chain's center link, and the bar half of the clasp.

8 Determine the finished length of your lariat's dangle. (This one is 7 in./18cm.) Cut a piece of chain to that length. Open a jump ring. Attach a leaf unit to one end of the chain. Close the jump ring. Continue attaching leaf units to the chain with jump rings, skipping one to seven links between units.

9 Open a jump ring. Attach the remaining end of the chain to the toggle clasp. Close the jump ring.

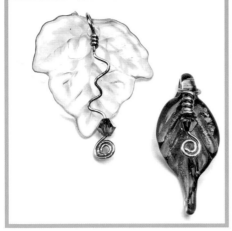

1 **earrings •** Make a wire spiral for two leaf-shaped beads. To make a wire spiral for a front-to-back–drilled bead, follow steps 1–4 of the necklace. To make a wire spiral for a side-to-side–drilled bead, follow steps 1, 5, and 6 of the necklace.

2 Cut a 1½-in. (3.8cm) piece of chain. Open two jump rings and attach a leaf unit to each end of the chain. Close the jump rings.

3 Open the loop on an earring wire and attach the dangle. Close the loop. Make a second earring to match the first.

Dangling drops

Lively crystal drops dangle from jump rings

by Fran Farris

Suspend jewel-tone drop beads from linked jump rings for a pair of deceptively easy cluster earrings. To vary the cluster's shape, use a smaller or larger jump ring – 4mm for a short, full earring or 5mm for a long, narrow dangle. After assembling your first pair, you won't even need the instructions.

SupplyList

- **18** 5 x 7mm Czech fire-polished crystal drop beads (Shipwreck Beads, 800-950-4232, shipwreckbeads.com)
- **18** 1½-in. (3.8cm) head pins
- **12** 4mm or 5mm jump rings
- pair of lever-back earring findings
- chainnose pliers
- roundnose pliers
- diagonal wire cutters

WIREWORK

1 String a crystal on a head pin and make a wrapped loop (see Basic Techniques, p. 6). Make 18 dangles.

2 Open a jump ring (Basic Techniques). String an earring finding's loop and two dangles on the jump ring and close it.

3 Open another jump ring. Link it through the previous jump ring, between the two dangles. String two dangles on the jump ring and close it.

4 Repeat step 3 twice.

5 Open a jump ring. Link it through the previous jump ring, between the two dangles, and close it. Open another jump ring and string a dangle. Link it through the previous jump ring and close it. Make a second earring to match the first.

Stylish wire ring

Create a fresh, fun ring with beads and wire

by Sara Strauss

Transform wire into a ring in a matter of minutes. Choose deep, rich colors, bright jewel tones, or pale pastels as you incorporate different beads into your design. You'll want to make many, so go ahead – each ring will take on a whole new look.

1 Locate your ring size on a ring mandrel and wrap a 3½-in. (8.9cm) piece of 18- or 20-gauge wire snugly around the mandrel.

2 Remove the wire from the mandrel and make a loop at one end.

3 Make a small half-loop at the end of a 6-in. (15cm) piece of 24- or 26-gauge wire and attach it to the ring, as shown.

4 Using either chainnose or bentnose pliers, hold the band in place. Make three or more wraps around the ring with the 24- or 26-gauge wire.

SupplyList

- **3** 3–10mm beads
- 3½ in. (8.9cm) 18- or 20-gauge dead-soft wire
- 6 in. (15cm) 24- or 26-gauge half-hard wire
- chainnose pliers
- roundnose pliers
- bentnose pliers (optional)
- diagonal wire cutters
- ring mandrel

5 String a bead and make three or more wraps around the ring. Repeat two more times.

6 Pass the wire up through the ring's loop.

7 Tuck the end of the wire under one of the beads. Trim the excess wire.

EDITOR'S TIP
For a thicker band, start with an 8-in. (20cm) piece of 18- or 20-gauge wire and wrap it several times around the ring mandrel. Use a 10-in. (25cm) piece of 24- or 26-gauge wire to attach the beads.

Hinged bangle

An art bead is the center of attention in this hinged bracelet

by Wendy Witchner

Keeping an art bead front and center on a bangle bracelet can be a challenge. By hinging the two wire pieces and shaping the bottom portion, the bead section stays where it will garner the attention. The hook-and-eye closure is placed inconspicuously opposite the hinge.

SupplyList

- 15–22mm art glass bead
- **2** 8mm accent beads
- **2** 4mm spacer beads
- **2** bead caps to fit art bead
- 12 in. (30cm) 24-gauge twisted wire (all wire from Thunderbird Supply Co., 800-545-7968, thunderbirdsupply.com)
- 5 ft. (1.52m) 20-gauge twisted wire
- 5 in. (12cm) 18-gauge plain wire
- 6 in. (15cm) 16-gauge plain wire
- chainnose pliers
- nylon-jaw pliers
- roundnose pliers
- diagonal wire cutters
- hammer
- bench block or anvil
- metal file or emery board

1 Cut a 5-in. (13cm) piece of 18-gauge plain wire. Fold the 24-gauge twisted wire in half and rest the fold on the plain wire. Hold the tail and half of the twisted wire tightly in one hand. With the other hand, wrap the twisted wire tightly around the core. After a few twists, hold the coiled wire with nylon-jaw pliers. When you've finished wrapping one end, repeat with the remaining wire, forming a 1½-in. (3.8cm) coil. (You'll use approximately 8 in./20cm of twisted wire to make 1 in./2.5cm of coil.) Slide the coil off the wire. Cut the coil into six ¼-in. (6mm) segments.

2 Make a 3mm-diameter plain loop (see Basic Techniques, p. 6) at one end of the 5-in. piece of 18-gauge wire. Slide a coil, spacer, coil, 8mm bead, coil, bead cap, art glass bead, bead cap, coil, 8mm bead, coil, spacer, and coil on the wire.

3 Bend the wire at a right angle at the end of the last coil. Bend the wire end around your roundnose pliers into a hook. Bring it around to meet the last coil; trim the wire at that point.

4 With roundnose pliers, bend ⅛ in. (3mm) of the wire back and pinch it flush against the hook.

5 Place the hook on a bench block or anvil. Hammer one side to strengthen it. Smooth the hook tip with a file or emery board, if necessary.

6 Place the bead section on your wrist. To calculate the length of the bottom section of the bracelet, measure the underside of your wrist from loop to hook of the bead section, leaving a little ease. Add 1½ in. and cut a piece of 16-gauge plain wire to that length. Make a plain loop at one end.

7 Wrap 20-gauge twisted wire on the 16-gauge core wire as in step 1. Work from the middle toward the loop, sliding the coil as necessary. Coil the second half of the twisted wire until the coil covers the core wire. Trim the excess twisted wire.

8 Open the loop on the bead section and link it to the bottom section's loop. Close the loop.

9 Place the bracelet around your wrist and shape it to fit comfortably. Determine where the closure loop should be to accommodate the hook. Cut the wires, allowing ¾ in. (19mm) for a loop. Trim the coiled wire so ¾ in. of the core wire is exposed. Make a plain loop in the same plane as the loop at the opposite end. Hammer the loop as in step 5.

SUPPLY NOTES:
Art beads in the bracelets on p. 68: Angi Graham of The Bluefrog Studio, 254-965-6005, bluefrog@ourtown.com. Art bead in the step-by-step shots: Heart Bead, 707-441-0626, heartbead.com.

Two-tone spirals

Create elegant spirals with two shades and textures of metal

by Wendy Witchner

Turn any bead into the focus for earrings or a pendant by surrounding it with a wire-wrapped spiral. Using silver wire for the wrapping with a gold-toned bead and core wire helps you create a versatile two-toned set.

Supply List

both projects
- chainnose pliers
- roundnose pliers
- diagonal wire cutters
- metal needle file

earrings
- 2 6–7mm beads
- 2 ft. (61cm) 18- or 20-gauge wire, gold filled, half hard
- 16 ft. (4.8m) 22-gauge wire, sterling silver, dead soft

pendant
- 6–7mm beads
- 1 ft. (30cm) 18- or 20-gauge wire, gold filled, half hard
- 8 ft. (2.4m) 22-gauge wire, sterling silver, dead soft

EDITOR'S NOTE
If your piercing holes are small, use 20-gauge wire for the core wire.

1 **earrings** • Cut a 12-in. (30cm) length of 18-gauge wire (core wire) and an 8-ft. (2.4m) length of 22-gauge wire (wrapping wire). Beginning 1½ in. (3.8cm) from one end of the core wire, coil the wrapping wire around the core wire. Continue coiling until you are about 2 in. (5cm) from the other end of the core wire.

2 Bend the 2-in. end of the core wire at a right angle ½ in. (1.3cm) from the end. Slide a bead on the core wire. Turn the end around the bead with roundnose pliers. Resume coiling until you reach the bead. Trim the excess wrapping wire.

3 Wind the wrapped wire around the bead two or three times, forming a tight spiral around the bead. Trim the excess wrapping if necessary. Press the spiral into a dome, with the bead in the front and the spiral receding.

pendant • Repeat steps 1 through 3 of the earrings. Bend the core wire next to the wire wraps at a right angle to the spiral. Trim the core wire to ½ in. and turn a plain loop (see Basic Techniques, p. 6) perpendicular to the spiral.

4 Use chainnose pliers to bend the core wire next to the wire wraps at a right angle to the spiral. Use roundnose pliers to curve the wire back down ¼ in. (6mm) from the coil. To keep the earring balanced, trim the tail of the wire at a point just lower than the bead. File the wire ends. Make a second earring by coiling the wire in the opposite direction to mirror the first.

Details

by Lea Rose Nowicki

Dress up common earring findings by wiring a bead in place

SupplyList

- 2 8-10mm glass beads or gemstones, horizontally drilled
- 2 3–4mm rice-shaped pearls
- 2 5–6mm rice-shaped pearls
- 6 4mm flat spacers with large hole
- 1 ft. (30cm) 24-gauge wire
- pair of lever-back earring findings
- chainnose pliers
- roundnose pliers
- diagonal wire cutters

Sometimes the smallest details add much more than expected to the finished piece. You'll never wear plain earring wires again.

1 Cut a 3-in. (7.6cm) length of wire and slide the large bead just past the center. Bend the wire so that the short and long tail overlap above the bead. Wrap the short tail tightly around the long one. Trim the wrapped wire close to the long wire tail.

2 Slide three spacers on the wire to cover the wraps.

3 String a 5–6mm pearl and make the first half of a wrapped loop above it (see Basic Techniques, p. 6). Slide the earring finding into the wire loop. Complete the wrapped loop.

4 Open the lever-back of the finding. Cut a 2-in. (5cm) length of wire and wrap it three times around the front of the finding near the bottom. Hold the first round in place with chainnose pliers while you're wrapping the second and third rounds.

5 Bring the wire to the front of the earring. Thread a small pearl on the wire.

6 Place the pearl against the finding and wrap the wire above the pearl three times. Trim the excess wire. Make a second earring to match the first.

Knotted jewelry can be simple and casual or intricate and refined. Is your preference bold leather or sleek satin? Perhaps you prefer rustic suede as your foil. In any case, knotting opens your options for both stringing material and bead choice. Don't be fooled by the complex-looking results; once you learn a few easy knots, you can combine them in a variety of ways to showcase special beads or create the perfect accessory for a new outfit.

Rings and fringe

Create a wild, free look with metal and leather

by Paulette Biedenbender

Inspired by the leather and metal look of motorcycle fashion, this necklace is more daring than demure, more carefree than conforming. The fringe can easily be added, along with crystals, to give the necklace some flash. If flash and fringe don't rev your engine, or if you're not the leader of the pack, eliminate the detailing and just go with the basics.

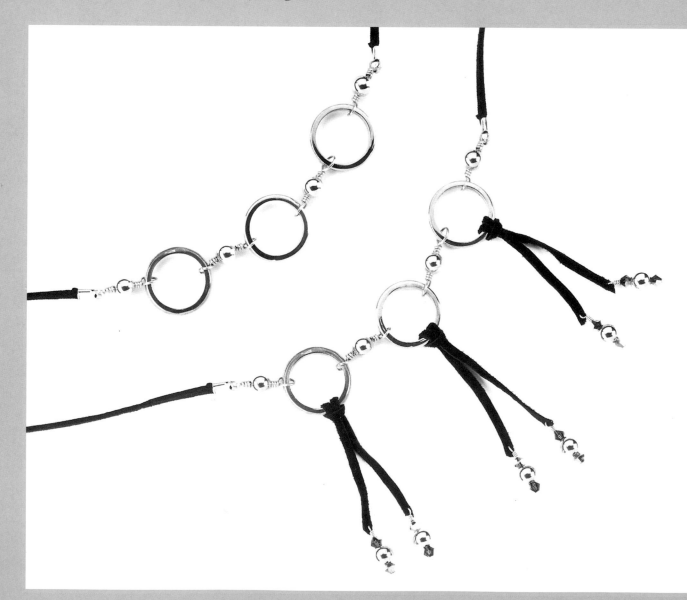

1 Cut four 3½-in. (8.9cm) lengths of wire. Make the first half of a wrapped loop (see Basic Techniques, p. 6) at one end of a wire and attach it to a ring.

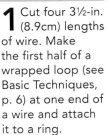

2 Finish the wrapped loop and string a 6mm bead onto the wire. Make the first half of a wrapped loop on the other side of the bead.

3a Slide a second ring through the loop and complete the wraps.

3b Repeat steps 1 through 3, until three rings are connected.

4 On each end ring, attach the wire and bead as in steps 1 and 2. Do not finish the wraps at the end of the bead.

Supply List

- **3** 22mm rings (Rio Grande, 800-545-6566, riogrande.com)
- **4–10** 6mm round beads
- **12** 4mm bicone crystals (optional)
- **12** in. (30cm) of ⅛ in. (3mm) suede lacing
- **12–18** in. (30–46cm) of 2mm Fashion Suede (Creative Beginnings, 800-367-1739, creativebeginnings.com)
- **14** in. (36cm) 20-gauge wire
- **6** 3-in. (7.6cm) head pins
- **4** crimp ends
- hook clasp and split ring
- awl or T-pin
- chainnose pliers
- roundnose pliers
- split ring pliers (optional)
- diagonal wire cutters

KNOTTING

5 Cut two 6 in. (15cm) strips of suede lacing. Attach a crimp end to each end of the suede (Basic Techniques). Repeat on the remaining suede strip.

6 Slide one crimp end loop into the wire loop and complete the wraps. Repeat on other side with the remaining suede strip.

7 To add fringe, cut three 6-in. pieces of fashion suede. Attach a piece to each ring using a lark's head knot (Basic Techniques). Trim the ends at an angle.

8 Use an awl or T-pin to make a hole ⅛ in. (3mm) from the end of the fringe. Repeat on the end of each fringe.

9 To make a dangle, string a 4mm crystal, a 6mm bead, and a 4mm crystal onto a head pin. Make the first half of a wrapped loop. Make a total of six dangles.

10 Insert a dangle into the hole on the fringe and complete the wraps. Repeat on the remaining fringes.

11 Open the loop of a hook clasp, attach it to one crimp end, and close the loop. Attach a split ring to the other crimp end.

Leather strung necklace

Use leather cord to display geometric beads

by Karin Buckingham

A mix of ceramic, gemstone, metal, or glass beads in geometric shapes is always alluring, but how can you show off the beads to their best advantage? This easy necklace of leather cord and wrapped loops showcases the sleek look of the beads while retaining a carefree appeal.

Supply List

- **2** 17mm flat squares, bronze (bronze and grenadine beads from Mykonos Beads, 888-MYKONOS, mykonosbeads.com)
- **17mm** flat square, grenadine
- **2** 10mm flat triangles, grenadine
- **25mm** donut, bronze
- **8** 10-15mm beads, bronze
- **1** yd. (.9m) wire, 22 gauge
- **3** decorative head pins, decoration larger than the bead holes
- **3** eye pins
- **1** yd. (.9m) 2mm-diameter leather cord
- clasp
- chainnose pliers
- roundnose pliers
- diagonal wire cutters

KNOTING

1 String a triangle-shaped bead, an eye pin, and a square-shaped bead on a decorative head pin.

2 Stack the beads, bend the eye pin at a right angle toward the back, and bend the head pin upward at a right angle.

3 Wrap the end of the eye pin around the bottom of the head pin, as in a wrapped loop, approximately ⅛ in. (3mm) above the wrap. Make a wrapped loop (see Basic Techniques, p. 6) with the head pin. Wrap downward until you meet the eye pin wraps. Trim the excess wire. Repeat steps 1 through 3 to make a second dangle.

4 Make a third dangle with a donut and a square in the same way.

5 Determine the finished length of your necklace. (This one is 16 in./ 41cm.) Double that measurement and add 4 in. (10cm). Cut a piece of leather to that length. Center beads and dangles on the leather as desired.

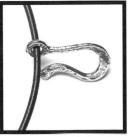

6 Center half the clasp on the leather to the right of the beads. Check the fit: When the center dangle is in place, the clasp should reach the middle of the back of your neck. Adjust the position of the clasp, if necessary.

7 Tie both strands in an overhand knot (Basic Techniques) to secure the clasp.

8 Bring the tail end of leather back toward the center beads and tie an overhand knot with both strands next to the last bead. Trim any excess leather. Repeat on the other end of the necklace with the remaining clasp half.

Simple and sophisticated

Combine leather and beads in a bold necklace

Men's jewelry should be bold but streamlined. Whether his style is natural or edgy, this design can be adapted to suit his unique personality.

by Naomi Fujimoto

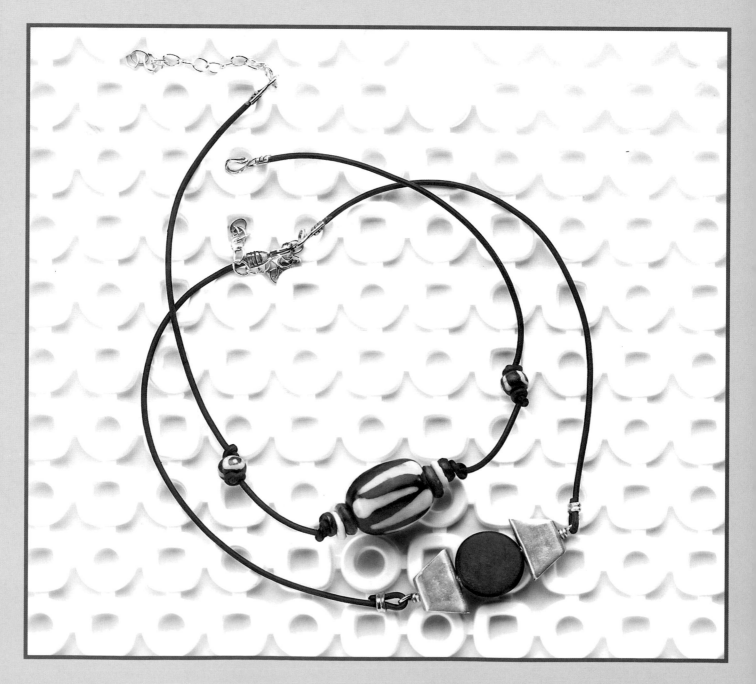

Each necklace is 16 in. (41cm) long and has a 3-in. (7.6cm) chain extender.

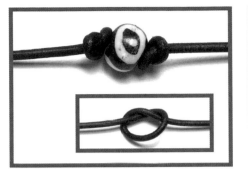

1 bone necklace • Tie an overhand knot (see Basic Techniques, p. 6 and inset) about 5 in. (13cm) or more from one end of a leather cord. String a round bead against the knot. Make a loose overhand knot close to the bead, slide the knot into position against the bead, and tighten the knot.

3a String three rings, a barrel bead, and three rings against the knot. Tie an overhand knot against the last ring.

3b Tie an overhand knot 1½ in. away, using the straw to space the knot, if desired. String a round bead and tie an overhand knot.

1 silver and wood necklace • Make a wrapped loop (Basic Techniques) at one end of the 20-gauge wire.

2 Tie an overhand knot approximately 1½ in. (3.8cm) away from the last knot. To make evenly spaced knots, string a 1½-in. piece of drinking straw flush with the knot. Tie a knot at the edge of the straw. Remove the straw. (Slit the straw, if necessary.)

4 Use a split ring to attach the clasp's loop to the chain segment.

5 Check the fit and cut the cord to the desired length on each end. Glue one end and insert it into the loop section of the clasp. Flatten the crimp section of the clasp with chainnose pliers. Attach the hook section of the clasp on the other end.

2 String a trapezoid-shaped bead, a circular bead, and a trapezoid onto the wire. Make a wrapped loop next to the end bead.

KNOTTING

SupplyList

both necklaces
- chainnose pliers
- split-ring pliers (optional)
- diagonal wire cutters
- E6000 adhesive
- drinking straw (optional)

bone necklace
- 20 x 24mm barrel-shaped bone bead (all beads in this article available at Planet Bead, 800-889-4365)
- **6** bone disk-shaped beads, **2** each of three colors
- **2** 7mm large-hole round bone beads
- 2 ft. (61cm) 2mm-diameter leather cord
- hook-and-eye clasp with crimp ends (Rio Grande, 800-545-6566, riogrande.com)
- 3 in. (7.6cm) chain (with large enough links for the hook clasp)
- 6mm split ring

silver and wood necklace
- 20mm circular wood bead
- **2** 13 x 20mm trapezoid-shaped metal beads
- 5 in. (13cm) or more 20-gauge wire
- 2 ft. 2mm-diameter leather cord
- **2** connectors (large crimps, Rio Grande)
- hook-and-eye clasp with crimp ends
- 3 in. chain
- 6mm split ring
- roundnose pliers

3a Cut two 10-in. (25cm) lengths of leather cord. String one piece through a connector, one loop of the beaded unit, and back through the connector, leaving a ½-in. (13mm) tail. Flatten the connector with chainnose pliers. Attach the remaining piece of leather to the other end of the beaded unit. Trim the excess leather.

3b Finish this necklace as in steps 4 and 5 of the bone necklace.

Masculine bracelet

Bone beads and leather cord combine for a casual bracelet

by Nancy Hoerner

This easy bracelet is made with traditionally masculine
materials. You can vary the amount of color and detail
in the bracelet with your choice of beads, cord, and
thread. It all depends on the comfort zone of the wearer.

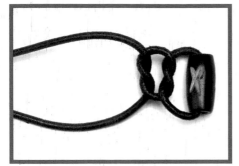

1 Determine the finished length of the bracelet. Measure the circumference of the wrist and add 2½ in. (6.4cm). (These bracelets are 9½ in./24.1cm.) Double that measurement, add 6 in. (15cm), and cut a piece of leather cord to that length. Center a bead on the cord and tie an open square knot (see Basic Techniques, p. 6).

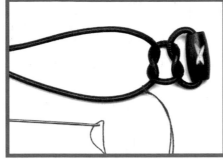

2 Thread a beading needle with 2 yd. (1.8m) of beading thread. Tie the end of the thread onto the cord near the square knot. Trim the excess thread.

SupplyList

- **26–30** medium oval horn beads, approximately 6 x 13mm (Fire Mountain Gems, 1-800-355-2137, firemountaingems.com)
- 1 yd. (.9m) leather cord, 1–2mm diameter
- 3–4 yd. (2.7–3.7m) beading thread
- diagonal wire cutters
- sewing or beading needle

KNOTING

EDITOR'S NOTE
Red beading thread was used in the step-by-step photos to make the process clearer, even though black thread was used to make the original bracelet dramatic. If you like the splash of color, stick with the red – or use any other bright shade. Beading thread is available by the spool at most retailers.

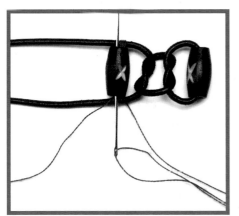

3 Position a bead vertically between the two pieces of cord. Bring the thread around the cord and through the bead four times.

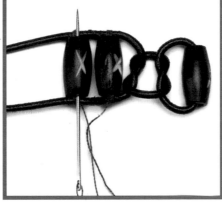

4 Place a second bead next to the first. Bring the thread around the cord and through the second bead four times. Repeat until the beaded cord is within 3½ in. (8.9cm) of the desired length.

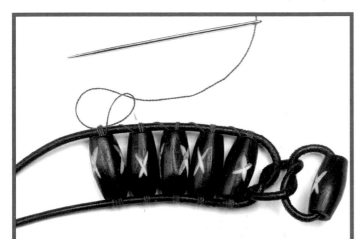

5 To tie off the thread, pass the needle between the thread and leather cord on one side of the last bead. Pull the thread so that a small loop is formed. Pass the needle back through the loop and tighten the thread. Repeat. Cut the thread ¼ in. (6mm) from the knot and tuck the end into the bead.

6 Tie a square knot. Tie a second square knot approximately ½ in. (1.3cm) from the previous knot. Tie the two cords together with an overhand knot (Basic Techniques) approximately ½ in. from the second knot. Trim the cord, leaving a 1-in. (2.5cm) tail.

Geode necklace

Put together a fresh necklace with a little slice of nature

by Naomi Fujimoto

Polished to perfection, geode slices are one-of-a-kind rocks with layers of crystallized minerals inside. You need not be a rock hound, however, to appreciate their beautiful concentric bands and translucency. For an unfettered look, string a geode on a yard or so of suede, wrap it around your neck, and tie a square knot. Now that's natural beauty.

KNOTTING

Supply List

- geode, approx. 25 x 35mm (Planet Bead, 800-889-4365)
- **4** 6–8mm washers, with holes large enough to accommodate suede cord
- 9mm or larger jump ring, to accommodate geode
- 3–4 ft. (.9-1.2m) suede cord, 3mm wide (Rupa Balachandar, rupab.com)
- **4** 4mm crimp ends (Fire Mountain Gems, 800-355-2137, firemountaingems.com)
- lobster claw clasp and **2** 6mm jump rings
- chainnose and roundnose pliers or **2** pairs of chainnose pliers
- diagonal wire cutters
- E6000 adhesive

1 Open a 9mm jump ring (see Basic Techniques, p. 6) and string the geode. Close the jump ring, being careful not to break the geode.

2 Determine the finished length of your necklace. (On this one, the strand with the geode is 14 in./36cm; each of the two remaining strands is 10¼ in./26cm, which leaves enough length to knot the ends.) Cut one piece of suede cord to the longer length and two to the shorter length, allowing ¾ in. (1.9cm) for finishing. Center the geode on the longer cord.

3 Attach a crimp end (Basic Techniques) to each end of the pendant's cord. Attach a crimp end to each end of the remaining cords.

4 Open a 6mm jump ring and string one end loop of the pendant strand, the loop of a remaining strand, and the clasp. Close the jump ring. Repeat on the other end, omitting the clasp.

5 String two washers on each of the remaining cord ends. Make an overhand knot (Basic Techniques) on each. Check the fit, and trim any excess suede from the knotted ends, if necessary.

Wrap necklace

Dangles and knots combine for a fun wrap necklace

by Paulette Biedenbender

There are times when you crave something out of the ordinary – whether it's an uncommon food combination, a sassy pair of sandals or a whimsical piece of jewelry. Indulgences can be quite energizing, so cast a strand of beaded suede around your neck and have fun.

Supply List

- 5 12mm glass beads, teardrop-shaped
- 4 10mm glass beads, round
- 8 8mm glass beads, round
- 1 yd. (.9m) suede strip
- 9 2½-in. (6.4cm) head pins
- 9 6mm split rings or soldered jump rings
- chainnose pliers
- roundnose pliers
- diagonal wire cutters

1 Center a split ring on the suede strip, fold the strip in half, and make an overhand knot (see Basic Techniques, p. 6) 1½ in. (3.8cm) above the split ring.

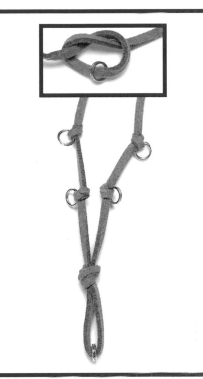

2 On each side of the strip, use overhand knots to tie on three separate split rings spaced 1½ in. apart (inset).

3 At each end of the suede strip, attach a split ring with an overhand knot. Tighten the knot close to the split ring. Trim any excess suede.

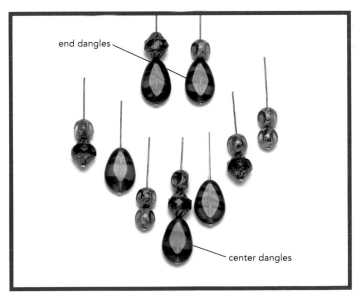

end dangles

center dangles

4 String a teardrop, a 10mm bead, and an 8mm bead onto a head pin to make the necklace's center dangle. String a teardrop and an 8 or 10mm bead to make each of the end dangles. Continue stringing one or two beads on each head pin in various patterns, one for each split ring on the necklace.

5 To finish the dangles, make the first half of a wrapped loop (Basic Techniques) above the top bead. Slide each loop into its corresponding split ring. Finish the wraps (Basic Techniques) on each dangle and trim the excess wire.

Classic knotted pearls

Create an elegant necklace with timeless appeal

by Lesley Weiss

A knotted strand of pearls is about as classic a necklace as you will find. Long considered the must-have item for any woman's jewelry wardrobe, pearls also have been revered as rare or expensive. With the wide variety of beautiful faux or freshwater pearls available today, however, there is no reason that every woman can't have a necklace in any color of the rainbow.

1a String a seed bead and go through it again, leaving a 4 in. (10cm) tail. Tie the tail to the working thread with a square knot (see Basic Techniques, p. 6). String a bead tip so that the two halves of the cup fit around the seed bead and knot. Close the bead tip with chainnose pliers. Trim the tail.

1b String two 2mm spacers and a flat spacer, three pearls, a flat spacer, two pearls, a flat spacer, and two pearls.

2a String an alternating pattern of one 4mm accent bead and three pearls, repeating the pattern seven times. String a 4mm bead.

2b String two pearls, a flat spacer, two pearls, a flat spacer, three pearls, a flat spacer, and two 2mm spacers to mirror the other end of the necklace. String a bead tip, hinged end first, and a seed bead. Slide all the beads toward the needle end of the cord.

KNOTING

EDITOR'S NOTE
These directions make a 15-in. (38cm) necklace. If you would like a longer necklace, add additional pearls and spacers to each end of the necklace.

3 Slide the first two 2mm spacers and the flat spacer to the closed bead tip. Make an overhand knot (Basic Techniques) and use an awl to position the knot next to the flat spacer. Slide the first pearl next to the knot. Make an overhand knot and slide it next to the pearl.

4 Continue making overhand knots between each bead, including a knot after the last pearl. Slide the spacers, bead tip, and seed bead against the knot, and tie the tail around the seed bead using a square knot. Trim the tail and close the bead tip.

5 Use roundnose pliers to roll the hook on the bead tip around the loop of half a clasp. Repeat on the other end with the remaining clasp half.

Net-wrapped pearls

Knot pearls in tulle for an up-to-date, two-strand necklace

by Paulette Biedenbender

Current fashion magazines show celebrities sporting a new twist on the multistrand pearl necklace. Knotted within tulle fabric, these high-quality pearls also carry a high-end price. You'll transform round pearls and off-the-bolt tulle into a lavish necklace without the lavish price; in sum, you'll be the one with celebrity appeal.

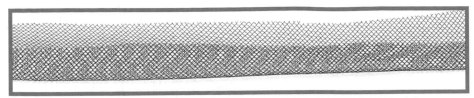

1a Determine the finished length of your necklace (the longer strand of this necklace is 18 in./46cm), double that measurement, and add 6 in. (15cm). Cut two strips of tulle to that length with a width 3½ times wider than the bead's diameter. Set one aside.

1b Fold the tulle into thirds, with each edge meeting the opposite fold.

KNOTTING

Supply**List**

- 21-in. (53cm) strand 6mm round Swarovski pearls
- 21-in. strand 10mm round shell pearls
- button with shank
- 1½ yds. (1.4m) tulle

2 Keeping the tulle folded, tie an overhand knot (see Basic Techniques, p. 6) 6 in. from one end.

3 To make the inner strand, insert a 6mm bead under one of the folds and slide the bead against the knot.

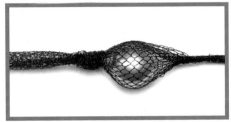

4 Overlap the opposite fold of tulle over the bead, and twist in the same direction as the top edge.

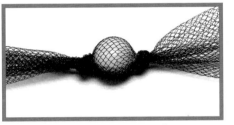

5 Tie a loose overhand knot, keeping the tulle twisted by pinching the fabric near the bead. Slide the knot against the bead and tighten.

6a Repeat steps 3 through 5. Check the length as you go until you are 1¼ in. (3.2cm) from the desired length.

6b To complete the outer strand, use 10mm rounds or a pattern of 10mm and 6mm rounds. Repeat steps 1b through 6a until you are 1 in. (2.5cm) from the desired length.

7 Match up the last knot on each strand and make a surgeon's knot (Basic Techniques) ½ in. (1.3cm) from the knots. Thread one strand of the tulle through the button's shank.

8 Tie a surgeon's knot on the other side of the shank, and trim the excess tulle ½ to 1 in. from the knot.

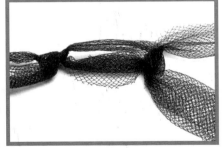

9 At the other end of the necklace, make a surgeon's knot ½ in. from the beads. Tie a second surgeon's knot, making a loop that will fit around the button. Trim the excess tulle ½ to 1 in. from the knot.

Sleek multistrand necklace

Sleek cording and cube-shaped Hill Tribes silver beads offer a contemporary combination

By Linda Augsburg

The playful, intricate look of this necklace is easy to achieve with simple overhand knots. The multiple strands of colorful cord and cube-shaped beads come together in an alluring, sophisticated arrangement.

1 a Cut three 6-ft. (1.83m) lengths of cord. Apply a thin layer of Fray Check to a ½-in. (1.3cm) section on the ends of each cord and let dry.

1 b String 14 or more beads on each cord. Set two cords aside.

3 a Slide a bead along one cord to the knot. Tie both cords in an overhand knot next to the bead, allowing space between the bead and the knots. Continue until the distance between the first and last knot is 6½ in. (16.5cm) short of the desired length of your necklace (this necklace is 19½ in./49.5cm long).

3 b Repeat steps 2 and 3 with the remaining cords. Cut each cord at the fold and slide off any extra beads. Tie a knot 1¾ in. (4.4cm) from the last knots on each end. Apply Fray Check to the cut ends.

2 Fold the cord in half. Tie an overhand knot (see Basic Techniques, p. 6) 3 in. (7.6cm) from the cut ends.

4 On one end, slide the cords in pairs through a crimp bead and flatten each crimp bead (Basic Techniques) ¼ in. (6mm) from the knot. Trim the cord near the crimp bead and apply Fray Check to the ends.

5 Cut a 4-in. (10cm) piece of wire. Form a hook at one end and loop it around the cord as shown.

6 Holding the tails with one pair of pliers, use the other pair of pliers to wrap the wire snugly around the tails. Bend the wire so it is parallel to the tails.

Supply List

- **42 or more** 8mm silver cube beads
- 2 4mm round beads
- 2 15 x 11mm beading cones
- 6 ft. (1.83m) each of three colors of 1mm-diameter cord (Mokuba New York, 212-869-8900, item number 0925, colors 9, 50, 57)
- lobster clasp and soldered jump ring
- 8 in. (20cm) 22-gauge wire
- 6 3mm x .082 in. crimp tubes (Rio Grande, 800-545-6566, riogrande.com)
- Dritz Fray Check
- chainnose pliers
- roundnose pliers
- diagonal wire cutters
- scissors

KNOTING

7 String a cone and a round bead onto the wire, hiding the tails of the cord in the cone and nestling the round bead in the cone's smaller opening.

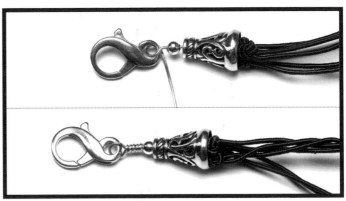

8 a Make the first half of a wrapped loop (Basic Techniques) ¼ in. above the bead. Slide the clasp on the loop and complete the wraps.

8 b Repeat steps 4 through 8a on the other end, using the soldered jump ring in place of the clasp.

Easy macramé choker

Combine cord and colorful beads for an easy-going necklace

by Karin Buckingham

This necklace uses a combination of overhand knots and a slight variation on the macramé square knot. Substitute beading wire for the center core cords in the macramé stitch, and you'll be able to include any accent bead you'd like – you're no longer limited to large-hole beads.

1a Determine the finished length of your necklace (this one is 15½ in./39.4cm). Cut a piece of waxed cord seven times longer than your finished length. Cut a piece of flexible beading wire 3 in. (7.6cm) longer than your finished length.

1b String beads in your desired pattern onto the flexible beading wire, beginning and ending with a crimp bead. Temporarily secure the ends of the wire with tape.

SupplyList

All necklaces
- 3 yds. (2.7m) waxed thread (The Leather Factory)
- flexible beading wire, .014 or .015
- 2 crimp beads
- scissors
- crimping pliers
- diagonal wire cutters

purple necklace
- **4** 15mm rectangular beads
- **6** 6mm round beads
- **10** 4mm bicone beads

green necklace
- **6** 12mm teardrop-shaped beads
- **5** 6mm cube beads
- **8** 4mm round beads, green
- **3** 4mm round beads, white

blue necklace
- **3** 10mm disc-shaped beads
- **5** 6mm round beads
- **8** 4mm round beads

KNOTING

2 Fold the waxed cord in half and tie an overhand knot (see Basic Techniques, p. 6), making a loop that is 7mm in diameter.

3 To make your necklace adjustable, tie two additional overhand knots, leaving a 7mm opening between each one.

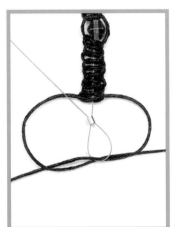

4 Make the first half of a macramé square knot (Basic Techniques) with the ends of the cord. Remove the tape from one end of the beading wire and wrap the wire around the crossed cord. Go through the crimp bead, and make a folded crimp (Basic Techniques). Make the second half of the square knot on the other side of the crimp.

5a Make ten alternating macramé square knots (five full knots). Slide a 4mm bead toward the knots, and secure with two alternating macramé square knots. Repeat with a 6mm and a 4mm bead.

5b Repeat step 5a, using a 15mm rectangle bead instead of the 4mm, 6mm, and 4mm beads.

6a Repeat steps 5a and 5b until the necklace is 2½ in. (6.4cm) shorter than your desired length. Make ten alternating macramé square knots.

6b Make the first half of a square knot. Loop the wire around the crossed cord and back through the crimp bead, as in step 4. Tighten the wires and make a folded crimp. Finish the square knot close to the crimp.

7 Make two overhand knots about 7mm apart for symmetry. String a 6mm bead on one cord, and make an overhand knot close to the bead. Trim the ends. Clasp the necklace by sliding the 6mm bead through the 7mm loop.

SupplyList

- 15 x 25mm dichroic glass bead with sterling loops (beads by Janet Wolery, available at Funky Hannah's Beads and Art, 262-634-6088, funkyhannahs.com)
- 16–18 in. (41–46cm) leather cord, 2mm diameter
- **2** crimp ends with loops, 4mm inner diameter
- **2** 4mm jump rings
- toggle clasp
- **2** pairs chainnose pliers or chainnose and roundnose pliers
- E6000 adhesive

EDITOR'S TIP
If the inner diameter of the crimp ends is too large for the leather cords, insert a ¼-in. (6mm) piece of leather into each crimp end before flattening it. The additional piece of leather will fill the extra space.

Dichroic glass bracelet

Tie leather cord to colorful glass for a hot, hip bracelet

by Anne Nikolai Kloss

Leather cord ties up an electric glass bead for a quick bracelet in three easy steps: Tie the cord in two lark's head knots, attach crimp ends, and add a clasp. Turn down the voltage with a dark-colored cord. Either way, this project is a painless way to unleash a little leather into your wardrobe.

1 Cut two 8–9 in. (20–23cm) pieces of leather cord. Fold one piece in half and string both ends through a loop on the dichroic bead. Bring both ends through the leather loop and tighten to make a lark's head knot (see Basic Techniques, p. 6). Make a lark's head knot with the other piece of leather on the remaining bead loop.

2 On one side, apply glue to the leather cord ends. Insert the ends into a crimp end. Flatten the crimp (Basic Techniques) with chainnose pliers. Repeat on the other side.

3 Open a jump ring (Basic Techniques). Attach the jump ring to one crimp end and to half of the clasp. Close the jump ring. Repeat on the other side.